MW01205600

...INSPIRED BY

Sri Mahavatar Babaji
Sri Amar Jyoti Babaji
Sri Paramhansa Yogananda

The

Eternal Question

Who Am I

by
Dharam Vir Mangla

M.Sc. M.Ed. PGDCA
Phone # +91-011-2242 9715
E-mail: dvmangla@hotmail.com
Website: www.geocities.com/godrealization

Edited by:
Raju Gupta
MCA

Winsome Books India

Paper-Back   ISBN # 81-88043-08-7

First Edition: 2004

Published by:
WINSOME BOOKS INDIA
209, F-17, Harsha Complex, Subhash Chowk,
Laxmi Nagar, Delhi-110092 INDIA
Phone: 22021284
· E-Mail: winsomebooks@rediffmail.com

If you feel this book is worth reading by others for the transformation of their soul, it will be a great service to God to recommend or gift it to your friends, relatives and seekers of God. There cannot be any other gift better then a book, which can bring eternal joy, bliss and happiness in their lives. The author will be pleased, if you mail your comments or any query to dvmangla@hotmail.com

CONTENTS

Dharam Vir Mangla

About the Author

Sh. D.V. Mangla, M.Sc. M.Ed. PGDCA got his masters degrees from university of Delhi. He belongs to a religious family. He is an extraordinary combination of spiritual & scientific bent of mind. He joined his Ph.D. in Mathematics at Delhi University in 1969. Since then he is practicing yoga and have the opportunity of the company and blessings of great saints. He used to discuss about God, *Shastras* and Science with saints and scientists. He has fully devoted his life in the pursuit of God, spiritual studies and yoga practices. He served as lecturer in Mathematics at University of Aden and worked as Principal in Delhi.

He is disciple of Paramhansa Yogananda and practicing 'Kriya Yoga' since long. He is a scholar of Science, Mathematics, Education and Philosophy. He has the ability to correlate Sciences, *Shastras,* Spiritual Science and God. His books are rare masterpieces based upon his spiritual experiences and vast studies and useful for believers and non-believers.

Besides his scientific-cum-spiritual discourses at various places and books, he also conducts seminars, workshops, for senior management and professionals on 'Reduce Stress through Self-Management and Positive art of Thinking'. These have drawn the attention of reputed institutions in India and abroad.

Sri Mangla is the founder of 'God Realization Foundation' (GRF) in Delhi. It helps the seekers of God to answer their personal queries and circulate the reply to all the members. On the basis of many e-Spiritual Tests conducted by the foundation members are accordingly advised for their eligibility of initiation in 'Kriya Yoga'. His writings are scientific commendable research work and a reservoir for further scientific researches.

Ashok Vardhan Dewan
Ex-Deputy Director Edu., J & K

A Word About the Book

The book has been written with the sole aim to serve the humanity & God. I have tried my best not to twist any spiritual, scientific and historical fact. Truth should never be twisted to please someone.

I have the blessings of the great saints like Sri Amar Jyoti Babaji, Mahavtar Babaji and Sri Sathya Sai Babaji. Generally the western authors are deprived of such opportunity.

I am thankful to Sri Amar Jyoti Babaji, a most revered saint of India, who has inspired and blessed me to write such books. All of my family members have his frequent company & blessings.

I can never forget the help of all the persons in publishing of this book.

Dharam Vir Mangla

PREFACE

This book is a unique & rare masterpiece, which help us to understand our basic nature, identity and existence of our real self. Since time immemorial we are haunted by the greatest eternal question 'Who Am I'. Nothing can be more important to us than to know and realize our lost identity and ownself.

The author explains scientifically and systematically that the whole universe/ creation is under great Illusion, Delusion & *Maya*. Whatever knowledge we gain through our finite mind and five senses is not an absolute truth, but a deceptive and false view as desired by God. Even the science is under the influence of *Maya*. Author has gone deeply into the subject 'Who am I' and has interestingly explained ego 'I', Knowledge-Information, *Ether*, Black holes, Dark matter & Dark energies, Neutron stars and Galaxies etc.

The subtle subjects like Dreams, Death and after Death have been explained scientifically and systematically. The author has explained various practical techniques of meditation for self-realization of our ownself and to know 'Who Am I'.

This book leads us from an insignificant human being to realize our basic identity that we are a drop in the Ocean of God i.e. 'Aham Brahmasmi' or 'That I Am' or 'So-ham'. It is useful for 'Soul Searchers'.

Dr. Archana Gupta
Director & Scientist 'E'
Council of Scientific & Ind. Research
Govt. of India, PUSA
New Delhi.

R.K. Gupta
Deputy Director General
National Informatics Centre
Govt. of India, CGO Complex
New Delhi.

**Photograph of Idol of Mahavtar Babaji at
Mahavtar Babaji Ashram, Kandwari, Palampur, H.P.**

1

Illusion, Delusion and *Maya*

ILLUSIONS

Unconceivable Triangle
which is not possible

Two horizontal lines
does not seem parallel

A young woman & an old
lady makes the illusion

If concentrate at the centre the
surrounding seems revolving
Our *Sahasrar Chakra* looks like it

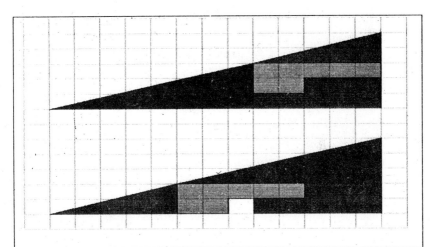

The shaded parts of two triangles are exactly the same. If you cut them out and re-arrange them like the second drawing, there remains a hole! How can this be?

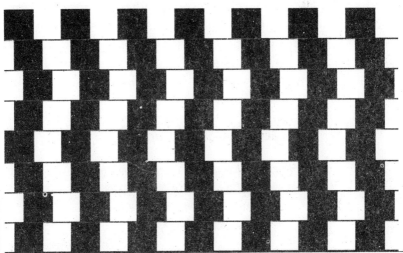

All the horizontal lines are parallel but appear to be inclined to each other

1

Illusion, Delusion and *Maya*
Prayer

O Divine Mother! Teach me to understand Thy great mystery of the spirit, mind, matter, energy and the wondrous universe around me. Since millennium and in my numerous past incarnations, I might have forgotten Thee, but I am sure, Thou art has not forgotten me even for an instant. Now I am in search of knowing Thy reality and nothing else. I am crying to find & meet Thou art since my first breath in Thy delusive universe. Father! By your *Maya* Thou hast separated me from Thee. I was busy with Thy enchanting creation and had forgotten Thee.

O Divine Father! Thy creation is already entrapped in Thy great Illusion, Delusion and *Maya*. Our limited senses, intelligence and mind do not perceive Thy absolute reality and Truth, but only glimpses of Thy great Dream-Drama projected through Thy Infinite Great Mind. O Creator of Lives! Help us to know Thy Drama.

Men's Unending Enquiry

Om Poornam-Madaa, Poornam-Midam,
Poornat-Poorna-Mudachiate;
Poornasia, Poorna-Madaya,
Poorna-Meva-Visisyiate.

                                    ... Isho-Upnishada

This means: O, God! Thou art infinite and complete. Out of Thy infinite formless existence, the infinite creation (universe) has come out from Thee as Thou manifestation. Thou art (the left-after) still infinite i.e. nothing has been reduced from Thee. Nothing can be added to Thee.

This nature of God exactly tallies with Mathematics. Mathematically this means if we subtract infinity from infinity it is still infinity and not less. ($\infty - \infty = \infty$). Conversely, if we add infinity to infinity it still remains infinity i.e. ($\infty + \infty = \infty$).

Since time immemorial the greatest puzzle of humanity has been to know our ego 'I', hidden in our physical body. All the western philosophies, physical & biological sciences have utterly failed to answer this mystical eternal question. But on the other side all the Hindu scriptures and the great Indian saints mainly concentrates to understand and to know our ego 'I'.

What is this 'I'? How to know this 'I'? What is that in our body, which is called 'I'? Is it a material or non-material thing? Who is the creator of this 'I'? What happens to ego 'I' at the time and after death? Where does 'I' go and remains after death? After how long time & how does our ego 'I' creates & select a new physical body for itself? Do we take birth in other living creatures. other then human? There are innumerable unanswered queries.

Why does it enjoy happiness & sorrows of life? Is there any way to make the ego 'I' free from the pangs of the cycle of life & death? How to get salvation and make ego 'I' free of births and deaths? What is death? Why and how our ego 'I' forcibly experiences the horrible dreams and creates another body during the dreams?

There are innumerable eternal questions, which are puzzling the minds of people who deeply think about life. To understand all these queries, first it is important to understand deeply the concept of Illusions, Delusions and *Maya*.

Since birth man observes so many illusions & delusions around him. His mind is generally befooled by his five senses & commonsense. He tries to understand all these delusions. To understand this there is a good example: man observes his own image hidden inside a plane mirror. His commonsense & mind interpret that the image is inside the mirror. After his investigation he finds that there is no such real image inside the mirror. A virtual image simply appears inside the mirror.

In fact no such image exist, and his mind wrongly interprets it as a real image inside the mirror. Since a mirror affects the minds of all the human beings and of all the animals for quite a long time, they think that there is no delusion in this phenomenon.

On the other side if the mind of an individual or a few persons misinterpret some phenomenon for a short duration of time, it is called an illusion. It is also interesting to understand misinterpretation done by the senses and mind.

After understanding following few examples you will be convinced to conclude that: "The information and interpretation reported by our sense organs and mind may not be absolutely correct. It is a misconception among most of the people that our five sense organs provide us knowledge of absolute truth".

What is an Illusion

Illusion means *'ill-vision'*. An error entertained by one or more persons (but not by the whole humanity) for a short duration of time is called *'avidya'*, or illusion. The person suffering from the illusion misinterprets the object. He can remove it by applying his own correct senses, reason, mind & intelligence. Illusion is not permanent. For examples:

- To presume a rope as a snake, by a person in the dark
- To presume a devil or some mysterious object, in the dark, which does not exist.
- A mirage of oasis in the dry desert etc.
- The color blindness and visibility of two or more objects instead of one due to defect of vision.
- Deceptive visions in illusion pictures.

It is clear and self-evident from illusion pictures (see) that the information reported by our eyes is not always correct. There are ultrasonic & supersonic sounds, in-numerable electromagnetic vibrations, cosmic rays; infrared & ultraviolet rays, microwaves, radio & T.V. waves and so many unknown waves around us. But our limited sense organs are failed to detect all these. Don't think that our sense organs observe the 100% correct information, but are able to observe only that which God has decided to observe for us under *Maya*.

The atoms and molecules of the whole universe, cannot arrange themselves of their own, to give the required shapes and forms to galaxies, stars, planets, living creatures, plants, animals, solids, liquids, gases and living creatures etc. It needs infinite intelligence of God to create and arrange all the microscopic particles, in the form as they are in the universe.

What is a Delusion

Delusion means '*dual-vision*' or 'diluted- vision'. It means seeing every thing apart from God. In delusion both ego 'I' and God exist. Delusion separates ego 'I' from God. The observer knows that every thing else is God, but still he feels his separation from God due to delusion. A delusion is an error entertained by the whole humanity for a long duration of time. Our intelligence, mind, senses and reason can partially interpret the phenomenons and the appearance of substances. But most of the time our senses report falsely. The correct scientific investigations and interpretations by our own intelligence can remove our delusion and inform us about the correct phenomenon or substance. A few examples of delusions are:

1. All human beings observe that *'Sun revolve around the earth'*. Which is false. In fact the earth revolve round the Sun and about its axis.

2. With our naked eyes the *stars look like the tiny bright objects suspended in the sky and appear a few kilometers away from earth*. In fact they are heavenly bodies like our Sun and are thousands of *light years* away from us.

3. Every body appears to fall towards the earth. But it is strange that the heavenly bodies like the stars, the sun and the moon do not fall on earth.

4. We feel that we are now observing the **present** positions of the stars like other objects. But in fact we observe them not of their present positions, but of many years past, depending on their distance. The nearest star we observe now is of at least four and half years before. The Sun we observe now is of 8 minutes and 20 seconds before as light takes this much of time to reach earth from Sun.

5. The surface of earth seems to be flat and at rest. In fact the earth is spherical and in motion. The Euclidian Plane Geometry, which we teach in our schools and colleges, is not true even on the surface of our earth. The sum of the angles of a triangle on the surface of the earth we live on

is not 180°, but more than 180°. Similarly the space around us is not linear as predicted by Einstein's General Theory of Relativity. Space has got a curvature due to gravitational field in it and the Euclid 3-D Geometry does not hold true exactly in space around us.

6. The color of the sky seems to be blue is an illusion. In fact sky has no color at all.

7. The depth of the bottom of a water tank looks less then the actual depth.

8. In a motion picture the motion of the image appears to be in continuous motion. In fact it is a series of still pictures projected more then sixteen images per second of a moving object.

9. There are all kinds of electromagnetic waves like Radio, TV, Wireless, X-rays, Ultra Violet, Infrared and Ultrasonic and microwaves etc. around us. But our five senses fails to detect these waves without proper scientific instruments.

Now it is clear that all these optical delusions are due to the misinformation or misinterpretation reported by our sense organs to our mind. From time immemorial the whole humanity has been suffering from all the above delusions. The science & technology are continuously helping us to understand and remove these delusions. It is significant to note that the human mind & intelligence is able to correct and remove these delusions.

We view the things around us according to our different mentalities and moods. Our eyes are unable to see the subtle astral bodies, aura around bodies and subtle astral colors, which are hidden in every thing around us. Our ears are

unable to hear the supersonic & ultrasonic sounds, astral
sounds and the *Anahat* sounds. Our nose is unable to smell
the astral fragrances due to its limitations. The taste of a
patient is changed during and after his disease. During the
paralysis the skin looses its sense of touch and the body does
not obey the orders of the mind. It appears that the sense
organs do not report the mind the absolute correct
information.

The diluted mind is not able to report the signals received by
it correctly to the ego 'I'. It is known as diluted-vision or
delusion. *We conclude that the whole humanity is under the
influence of delusion.*

What is *Maya*

But *Maya* is different to some extent from illusion &
delusion. *Maya* is our ignorance and a cosmic delusion
created by God. It is a cosmic force by which *Brahman* has
separated Himself from His own creation. The power of
consciousness to separate & divide is called *Maya Shakti*.
Before the creation of universe God, was alone. When God
started the creation, He became the Creator.

All our educational systems, throughout the world are simply
busy in studying and getting more & more information or
Vidya (limited knowledge) about the creation and ignoring
the Creator. Sciences & Technologies can simply answer the
how of a question but ignore the *why* of question. The Creator
is waiting, whether his best creation the human beings will
ever start thinking about their Creator?

Our universe is not an ultimate reality, but it is just the God's
dream or a thought of His Mind. God is dreaming the dream
of cosmic motion pictures on the delusive human

consciousness. *Maya* is responsible for the manifestation of 'formless' God to provide different "forms". *Maya* reduces the omni powers of Cosmic Consciousness to limited existence of matter, mind, intelligence and soul. Due to Maya we have forgotten that we were God in the beginning and we will again merge in God in the last. Due to *Maya* we also feel our association with the ego 'I'.

Engrossed in the illusions and delusions of the universe, we are unable to see the hidden tricks of *Maya*, which it plays on our senses. We are already trapped and captured by the enchanting temptations of the illusory world, and get caught in sensual pleasures. It leads us to the tragic realm of innumerable births and deaths.

A **self-realization** is waking up from the illusion, delusion and *Maya*. A self-realized yogi realizes that the entire cosmos and the universe lie within him. He becomes one with God permanently. It is an *involutionary* step back to God by the human soul. Soul looses its own entity merges with God. The ego 'I' melts away in Ocean of God.

The universe is just a great thought in the mind of God. If God just stops His dreaming, the universe will dissolve immediately in God. For a child the motion pictures on television screen appears to be true and real, but that the pictures on television screen are only images created by light and nothing more. Similarly the universe is just a motion picture or a dream of God on a four-dimensional screen of space & time by a universal hidden projector.

For a dreaming man the dream appears to be a total reality. The dreaming man forgets every thing of his awakened universe and even the existence of his physical body in this world. As man has got the power to dream and to create his own dream universe, similarly our universe is simply a great dream of God and its creatures are just active images or simply puppets in His Universal Dream.

The following *fundamental law* is acceptable to both the physical and spiritual sciences: *'if there exist anything, it must have been created by someone and cannot come into existence itself out of nothing. There cannot be anything without any creator or without any cause.'*

Another *fundamental law* acceptable to both is the **'Law of Cause & Effect'** i.e. *to every effect there must be a cause.* If there is any thing in the universe it must have been created by some one. Nothing can be created out of nothing. Even the thoughts coming to the mind must have a cause. Thoughts cannot come out of nothing. How the thoughts are coming to our mind? What the science has done in this regard?

A Thing Exist only if Its Thought Exists in the Mind

We know that from the beginning of the universe, there exist cosmic rays, X-rays, radio waves, gamma-rays; electro-magnetic, gravitational and magnetic fields & micro waves; hundreds of fundamental atomic & subatomic particles of matter & anti-matter and all the laws of natural sciences governing this universe including our earth.

But until few hundred years ago, man was not even aware of any of these things. And a few hundred years back there was no existence of all these things in the mind of man at all. If some one or a scientist or a saint or any body else, would have talked about the existence of these things, he might have been humiliated, punished or hanged or become a laughing stock in the world. Accordingly so many people have already faced and suffered the cruelty of world in the past history. All the above scientific findings do not exist even today or have any meaning, in the minds of the millions of illiterate people and other living beings.

For example: If some body has not heard or has no concept of bacteria, virus, atoms and subatomic particles then all such things does not exist in his mind for him. Even today we may not know about so many wondrous things already existing in the universe about which we are not aware of. Daily we experience that during our sleep and dream this world does not exist at all. The thought of this illusive world melts away while we dream during sleep.

At a particular instant of time we are aware of only a single thought existing in our mind at that particular instant of time. We forget the rest of the things of the universe & even our physical body at that instant of time. We have only one mind and can have only one thought at a particular instant of time, in our mind.

Our past concepts about the soul, physical body, matter and the universe are constantly & rapidly changing. After so many achievements, can we claim that nothing more is left to find about? Absolutely not. Un-till now we have found only a few things out of the infinite unknown things. Is there any way to find out and know everything instantly at a time, in our lifetime?

As per the *Vedas & Shastras,* you may not believe that, *the answer is 'yes'.* Accordingly, there is a big difference in the mind & intellect of human, as compared to all other living beings on earth. Similarly there is a big difference in the mind and intellect of man, as compared to the Cosmic-Mind and infinite intelligence of God.

God has given only to man the power to think about Him but to none else. Would you believe that after self-realization, a man become one with God and he achieves everything, including all the super-powers of God?

Maya is different from an illusion or delusion. Maya cannot be removed by our human intellect and without the grace of God. The human mind & intelligence is not able to overcome & remove the ignorance due to Maya. *Maya is the power of God, which creates an illusions and delusions, to separate the creation from the creator.*

We know fog vanishes before the Sun. Similarly our ignorance due to *Maya* vanishes before the knowledge of God. We remove the husk that covers the rice or wheat. Similarly we remove the ignorance, delusion and *Maya* that adheres to the mind of man, by the regular practice of meditation, introspection and *samadhi*. During *samadhi* we realize the absolute truth and knowledge face to face and nothing else is needed to explain.

General Knowledge Tests
Are not the Tests of Knowledge

All over the world in almost all the countries there are General Knowledge Tests and there are thousands of books written on General Knowledge for the preparation of these tests. In fact neither of these tests measure knowledge nor the books are about General *Knowledge*. In fact all these books and tests are about General *Information* only. These tests simply measure the information stored in the mind of the candidates by his power of cramming the information.

A really knowledgeable man like a great scientist or a saint or a writer may utterly fail in these information tests. Does it mean that they do not have General Knowledge? The incorrect name of these tests misleads our students about the correct concept of knowledge. So our educationists should do something to change the name of these tests to avoid confusion between the meaning of words knowledge and information. You will agree that nearly all the researches and discoveries in the field of sciences are information only.

Difference Between Ignorance, Information and Knowledge

Information is the data that the scientists, the educationists, the teachers and other agencies are supplying to us about their studies of **creation** around us and is mostly transferred to the students, through their teachers in our universities, colleges and schools. The media is also a good source of supplying the information.

But the data that remove our ignorance due to *Maya* and lead us more and more nearer to God or to better understand God and our ownself is called **knowledge**. While the data, which creates more confusion, and lead us away from God i.e. to deny the existence of God, is called **ignorance**. Most of the times the same data is interpreted in different ways by different people. It may become **knowledge** or **ignorance** as per their interpretations.

Bhagwad Geeta, Shastras and Bible are the good source of knowledge of God and our soul. So these are the ocean of knowledge and not mare information. The events stated about a war in newspapers and the contents given in general knowledge books or tests are only information. There is Ministry of Information or education in most of the Governments, but there is no Ministry of Knowledge in any Government.

As fog disappears before the Sun, ignorance melts away before the knowledge. The divine knowledge is acquired by constant meditation upon God. We can remove all our doubts by consulting the self-realized saints and our Guru. When our ignorance due to delusion disappears, our true Self *(Atma)* shines in its own splendor.

The Knowledge of God
Is Self-Explanatory & Self-Evident

A blind man by birth can never understand the true nature of light. However we may try our best to explain, define and clarify about the light to a blind man, it will be all in vain. A blind man by birth will never be able to understand light however efforts we do. He will always think that we are just befooling & wasting his time.

But if anyhow, we are able to show him the actual light and the glimpse of our world for few seconds, it is sufficient for him to understand light & its importance without any further explanation. Similarly a dumb & deaf man by birth cannot understand the concept of sound till he listens the sound. Hence, God has made things self-explanatory.

The conflict between believers and non-believers of God is never ending. The believers declare that God is to be found at this place and everywhere. The non-believers says that God can be found nowhere at any place. This fight between the two has been throughout the past ages.

Our two eyes give us the view of the vast expanse of the universe and space; but our eyes cannot see our own face to which they belong, without a mirror. However the two eyes are the part of our body, the eyes cannot see the back and the inner parts of our body. Even the outer and inner visible parts of our body do not look same as visible through powerful microscopes.

Whatever is visible through naked eye is an illusion or delusion, not the absolute reality. The spiritual science tells us the ways to get rid of these illusions and delusions. Therefore a person who has no experience and knowledge of spiritual science and divine concepts cannot comprehend God even if he is a scientist.

Our eyes can see but cannot talk or hear. Our tongue can talk but cannot see or hear. Similarly our ears can hear, but cannot talk or see. No sense organ can do the work of the other organ sense organ. God and the Divine can be grasped only through universal love, through faith, through devotion and true *sadhna*. Love and devotion unites us with God, but *Maya* separates us from God.

To verify the truthfulness of God or the *Shastras*, the scientists have to strictly follow the spiritual laws. Even if they fail to verify, there is something lacking in their *sadhna or practice,* but not in God.

We have been born inside the universe and the omnipresent *ether*. We can never understand both these fully, unless & until: we observe both of these from outside the limits of the universe or become one with the ether and the universe. To understand this think of a fish, which is born inside the deep bottom of sea, and has never come out of the seawater in its lifetime, to look the outside world or the universe. Such a fish can never understand the presence or the existence of seawater around it and the universe out side the water.

Similarly we are born inside the omnipresent *ether* and the vast universe and we can never go out of the universe & *ether*. According to spiritual science, the universe and *ether* are inside our mind. During meditation we can go beyond our mind and then we can understand both the universe and the *ether*. Do not doubt upon this.

As per the famous French Mathematician Rene Descartes, if human can conceive the idea of God, God must then exist, for whatever the brain can think of must have a basis in Truth. *"A clear and distinct idea of an absolutely perfect Being contains the notion of actual existence; therefore since we have an idea of an absolute perfect Being such a being must really exist."*

Remember: "Our proud of little learning and sallow knowledge is our biggest enemy, to learn more and to know the absolute reality of the universe. Through the science whatever we have learnt or learning is only about the creation. It is just a glimpse of the dream of God, which provides a little information about him. The whole universe and all the creatures are the images and like puppets on a 4-dimentional screen of space and time, projected by a universal stereoscopic holographic projector in the mind of God. Due to Maya, we are misinterpreting the dream images as the reality, which is false."

Om Anandam Om

2
The Eternal Question
Who am I

Prayer
Who Am I
We are living alone in the Crowd
How Can We Know our Ego 'I'
Strange Personalities in the World
Story of Shepherded Lion Cub under Delusion
Scientists have No answer to queries of a Child who Wonders
    His Mysterious Physical Body
All Fundamental Elementary Particles are Exactly Alike
The Universe is Made Up of Only One Material
Do we Know Completely about Anything
Wonderful Arrangements of Atomic & Subatomic Particles
Microscopic View & Macroscopic View of Creation
Concept of Universe is Different in Different Minds
About the Sleep, Dreams & Death
Any Desire at Death is the cause of Rebirth
The Great Dreamer of the Future of World Nostradamus
Universe is Not Eternal
Brahman is the Only Reality
Neutron Star is the Condensed Form of the Dieing Matter
Black Holes are the Mouths of God to Digest the Creation
Newly Discovered *Dark Matter* and *Dark Energies*

2
The Eternal Question
Who am I
Prayer

O, Divine Consciousness! O, Ocean of Bliss! Since millennium I do not know myself, because I have forgotten Thee due to my ignorance. I am taking pangs of joy and sorrow, life after life and from birth till death. The greatest ignorance puzzling me throughout is: Who am I? I have realized that I am neither the physical perishable changing body, nor I am brain, nor the life force, nor I am mind, nor I am intelligence and nor the thoughts. Also I can never be anything, which belong to me and is mine. I am the king of all such things.

O Mother Divine! In the false changing world everything is changing continuously, but my ego 'I' remain the same throughout my life in the same body. I am the same witness & the same observer during my awakening, sleep, deep-sleep and meditation states of consciousness. I am eternal, unchangeable, imperishable immortal and deathless soul.

O Giver of our life & death! From where do I come in this world? Where will I go, after my death? Why I have to experience the horrible dreams during my sleeps? Why I do not have a freedom to decide to have a body of my own choice and sweet will? Why my birth and death are not in my control? Why I am made sick all of a sudden without my will and how I am cured of the diseases without my knowledge? How can I remove the ignorance of my soul to know who really I am? What is my relation to Thee?

The Eternal Question
Who am I

This is the greatest puzzling question, which is haunting the whole humanity since time immemorial. Can there be anything more important than to know our ego 'I' or who am I? From where I came to this earth and where will I go after my death? Who gave me this body and forced me to live in it? Do I have any freedom in selecting a suitable body of my own choice and design? For how much time, I will have to remain in this body?

Such questions are hunting the mind of the seers. The humanity on earth has always been busy in learning about the history of creation, solving the human problems & sufferings and to understand the mysteries of the universe, but ignoring the above puzzling questions.

We know only a little bit of our body, but do not know any thing about our ego 'I'. We are sure that we possess a physical body and there is an ego 'I' which exist in our body. Our ego 'I' is the most important thing among all, in this universe. We can sacrifice any material thing even the dearest thing for the sake of this 'I'. Since birth our ego 'I' is trying to learn about so many things of the universe including the great puzzle '*Who am I*'? This is the question where the sciences and philosophies have not helped much. But the holy Vedas & *Shastras* begins with this basic question.

There have always been some changes in our body since our birth. Science has informed us that some new cells are replacing all the present cells of our body after some time. It means we have an entirely new body made up of new atoms, molecules and cells after some time.

But our ego 'I' does not change in the new body. Our ego 'I' remains the same in our body throughout our life, till death. No other 'I' of someone else, can replace our ego 'I' during our lifetime in our body and vice-versa. Due to *Maya* we are completely ignorant & have forgotten about our own 'I'. We don't know from where this 'I' came? What shall happen to this 'I' after my death? Will 'I' exist after my death or not? Who gave me this body and forced me to live in it and to act in the world? Why I am forced to dream the dreams, I don't like? Why do I suffer and made sick? Why I have no complete freedom & always happy? What is the real source of my happiness?

Ego 'I' is associated with a body, it may be a physical, astral, ethereal or any thing else. Ego 'I' cannot exist without a body. Even during our dream our physical body is kept lying in the physical world but ego 'I' creates another body to act for. The dream body is not made from physical matter. Even after our death Ego 'I' leaves the physical body and creates another body made from astral matter and remains in the astral world for some time. If ego 'I' doesn't possess a body means its death and then it merges with God from where it has been originated. Our ego is like a droplet of water in the ocean or the vast infinite God. God originates the droplets of souls and merges back the droplets after some time.

As due to the fast turbulent motion in the ocean infinite waves, bubbles and drops are created. Similarly when the turbulent Cosmic Kundalini energy works in the ocean of Brahman, it creates infinite souls each with an ego 'I'. As a drop of water is not different from the ocean, similarly our soul with ego 'I' is not different from God. Only *Maya*, which creates ignorance, has separated both. If anyhow we can remove the ignorance due to *Maya* we can go back or merge ourselves in God. This is the ultimate aim of life. This aim can be achieved either in one life or in so many lives. One should never be disappointed for delay and do his best efforts to achieve salvation for his soul.

All the souls have come from God and naturally each soul is also willing to go back to its original source. All the creation has also come out of God and ultimately the whole creation will merge back in God at the end of the universe. Anything, which has taken birth, must die one day. Anything, which has been created with a purpose, must go back to its source after the purpose is achieved. Even the religions, which have taken birth and are man made must end one day. A few hundred or few thousand years are insignificant in the vast billions of year's time of the universe.

We are Living Alone in the Crowd

We have to accept that we are living 'alone in the crowd'. You may be living along with your spouse, children, parents, brothers and sisters or friends. But all are individually living alone in their aloneness. You are also living alone in your aloneness. No other being can touch the aloneness of any body else. If you want to know yourself you will have to learn the art of 'living alone in the crowd'.

It is your delusion or misconception that you believe that you know the persons with whom you are living along and the others should also know you. It is also false to say that your spouse should know you very well. Nobody knows you exactly, even you. You also don't know any body exactly. It is not possible to know others. We all are strangers to each other in the perishable and changeable world. It is due to the fruits of our past actions (*karmas*) that we have come together and are playing our part in the great universal drama. Is there any way to know others & us? Really there is.

How to Know Ego 'I'

If we want to understand our ego 'I', then our own 'I' should become the object to be known and the observer also. Remember our ego 'I' is not our physical body. It is different from physical body. Our 'I' do not possess any sense organ, brain, mind or intelligence. 'I' is different from physical matter even the *ether*. In the process of knowing our ego 'I': 'I' become the object to be known, and 'I' become the observer & also 'I' becomes the senses to report. When all these three become one during our meditation state, we can know ego 'I'. In this state there are no sense organs functioning, no vibrations emitted by the object, no brain, no mind, no intelligence, nor anything else.

When the object, senses and the observer become one, then and then only we can understand our ego 'I'. When you are really alone in a perfect silence you can know yourself. But it needs the grace of God also.

Do not allow your mind to read and watch everything and anything by everybody. Do not watch any silly thing broadcasted on TV by others. Avoid gossiping any stupid talks with anybody. Do not waist your *prana* in rubbish talks and discussions. Your mind is already burdened with so many rubbish thoughts and memories. It needs cleansing and unburdened by your deep meditation.

Through yoga practices and deep meditation, you will experience *Samadhi* one day and your *Kundalini*[1] will be awakened. Samadhi & the awakening of the Kundalini are the door & beginning of your journey to know ego 'I' and God also. Your journey back to God will start. It is known as the process of *involution*. Yoga is a broad term it does not mean simply asanas as propagated by quacks.

Strange Personalities in the World

To understand our ego 'I' it will be better, if you understand first the following few interesting examples of strange personalities in the world. The *Puranas* and the Holy books are also full of such strange personalities:

➤ Some individuals have been found with two or more brains instead of ordinarily one brain. They can do two or more different works at the same time. At present there is a lady who can write two different letters with her two different hands at the same time. But she has only one ego 'I' in her personality. Ravana is said to have ten brains and ten minds in a single body.

➤ Some snakes and some extra ordinary persons have been found with two or more heads in a single body. The famous Lord *Seshnag* (The King of snakes) is said to have one thousand heads. Most of the Hindu Gods have more then one head on their body. But all of them have single ego 'I' in their personalities?

➤ There are examples of twins having two heads with only one lower body. They have two different egos 'I' sharing one physical body.

---

[1] For detail read 'Kundalini & Kriya Yoga' & 'God & Self-Realization' by Dharam Vir Mangla

➤ There are historical examples that an advanced yogi leaves his old diseased body and enters his ego 'I' in the body of some other dead body of healthy young man. Mysteriously the dead body of the young man became alive with a different ego 'I' of the yogi. The yogi lives his later life comfortably in the new body of the other person.

➤ The Hindu *Puranas* and many others are full of miracles that some of the men were able to transform their body into any other form of different creatures at their will. It is said that even some of the snakes have this power to assume any form of any creature, even the human form.

➤ But there is not even a single example that the ego 'I' of a man in his body is changed during his life. There are changes and variations in the physical body throughout the life, but the ego 'I' remains unchanged. Since it is immortal and eternal. No scientific theory of evolution can explain, how this ego 'I' was evolved in the living beings or in the living organism.

The Story of a Shepherd Lion Cub
Under Delusion

There is a good illustrative story from great saint Kabeer of India about the ignorance of our soul: Once there was a shepherd in a village. One day he caught a young lion cub in the forest. He brought the cub to his house and kept him among his sheep. In sort time the lion cub learned mixing with other sheep and acquired all the traits of sheep. He used to love, play, eat and sleep with them. He became teetotaler, coward and non-violent.

As the lion cub grew up, due to his ignorance he forgot that he was a lion. He was convinced that he was also a sheep like others. After few years the lion cub became a full grownup lion, even then he began to behave like a coward and a non-violent vegetarian sheep. He had lost all his original characteristics and qualities of a lion in the jungle.

After some time a full-grown up lion came to the village from the nearby forest & met the lion living with the shepherd. The lion of the forest wondered & shocked to know that a full grown up lion like him was behaving like a coward sheep and was also a vegetarian & non-violent. Immediately he understood the cause of his strange behavior. He tried to convince him that he was a lion and not a sheep. He tried his best to remove his delusion and ignorance of shepherded lion but failed.

Then he asked the shepherd lion to accompany with him inside the forest, where there were many other lions. When the shepherd lion saw the other lions of the forest, enjoying, killing, eating other animals, he at once realized his ignorance, laughed at his own folly. He changed immediately into a strong and normal lion like others. After that there was no need to teach him that he was not a sheep, but a lion.

In the same way the human children are brought up with the men, who are ignorant about their real nature of soul or God. The children associate themselves with their physical body and behave like an ignorant man when grown up. But when an ignorant man met with a self-realized Guru, who removes his ignorance and *Maya*, and make him to realize that he is infinite, immortal & cosmic consciousness and not the perishable body. He makes him convinced that his soul is nothing but God. His ego 'I' and God are the same. Only

Maya has separated both. You now have a little glimpse of your ego 'I', but still you have not realized the truth of it.

Bible in Genesis 1:26 also says "Let us make man in our image" When God created man He created him in His image. Psalm 82:6 also gave the same statement "You are gods. You are all children of the Most High." When Moses saw the burning bush, he asked, "If the people asked me what is your name, what shall I tell them?" God answered, "I AM THAT I AM."

This is same as per Vedas: "*Soham*" or "*Tatvamasi*". Our ego 'I' is the micro 'I am' of God. Our body is not the soul nor 'I am'. Nor it is mind, nor intelligence. Our body is simply the temple to live in and an instrument to act in the world.

Scientists have No Answer to so many Queries of a Child who Wonders his Mysterious Physical Body

How do the illusion, delusion and *Maya* affect our understanding of the universe? When a child is born, he takes his first breath in the world, he cries, because he has been imprisoned in a physical body.

A child is surprised to know that he possess a physical body. His body has some of the basic needs to sustain, depending upon the outside world. He has no knowledge, who has given him his body and why it has been given to him? He knows that he has not come to this world out of his own choice and will. It appears that a super-power has imprisoned him in his physical body to achieve His hidden objective from him. What does He want from him? Science has yet to answer to these queries.

It is observed that a newly born baby has already learned so many hereditary behaviors, without learning them from outside world. Since birth the baby knows how to breathe, how to drink, good or bad tastes, how to smile & weep, instinct of hunger & excretion, sleeping, sense of touch & pain and so many inherited human behaviors. Is it not miraculous, how a child learns, all these inborn human behaviors? Science has yet to do further research work to answer these questions.

Further as the body of a child grows he realizes that there exist a mysterious and a wonderful universe around him. His little mind is unable to understand & grasp the delusion and *Maya* around him. He is unable to understand his mysterious and wonderful physical body, the people, the world and the universe around him. He tries his best to understand the universe, the different organs of his body and their functions inside and also about the world outside his physical body. But his little intellect fails to answer his numerous queries.

Due to delusion a child observes that every thing falls from above to below. But he does not understand why the heavenly bodies like the sun or moon or stars do not fall on the ground? He also does not understand why earth attracts every thing? What is the cause of gravitational force? How do actually the two heavenly bodies attract each other from such a great distance?

Do the science really knows the cause of gravitational force of attraction & how actually the gravitational forces affect the other bodies in the universe till now? Why the gravitational force has no repulsive force, like magnetism and electricity?

What exactly causes two heavenly bodies to attract each
other at an enormous distance of billions of light years?
What really is a gravitational field? What changes it brings
in space between the two bodies? Is there any kind of
exchange of gravitational particles called *gravitons*, which
are still unknown to science?

Just like gravitational field we also do not know much about
electric and magnetic fields. All these 'fields' are still
mysteries for us. Till now we simply know the
mathematical formulae searched by Newton or Einstein
about the gravitation, nothing more.

Regarding his little physical body a child wonders as: Who
is palpitating his heart, which needs a tremendous amount
of constant energy? Neither he can stop it nor he can run it
at his own command and will. His heart is functioning
regularly without any break since his first breathe in the
world and it will continue palpitating till death. He has no
control over his heart.

His stomach or his digestive system is digesting all kinds of
food, which consists of millions of complex chemicals. His
body is manufacturing thousands of complex chemicals,
needed for its sustenance, without his slightest knowledge
of these chemicals & their need? He has absolutely no
control and no knowledge of thousands of complex
chemical actions and reactions, taking place in his small
compact body. Most of the time he is not even aware of his
body at all, as during the sleep.

A child further wonders after knowing that there is a
world's biggest industry of manufacturing complex
chemicals and thousands of organs are functioning in

perfect order in his small body. He also learns that he has many wonderful net works of sense organs, which produces special signals & report the information received by them instantaneously to his brain.

But he fails to understand how these complex signals of sense information are reported correctly to the brain? How his brain further interprets them correctly & reports these signals to his mind? And how his mind further reports these signals to his ego 'I' instantaneously? Does science know the answers of these till now?

Sense organs produces → special signals → transmit signals through network of neurons & nerves → reports to special faculty in the brain → brain interpret signals & report further to the Ego 'I' i.e. the soul → soul is the ultimate observer, which records & experiences all kinds of signals → soul further stores these experiences in its memory and has the ability to recollect the experiences from its memory space.

Due to *Maya* a child is ignorant and has no knowledge of the exact happening of all these phenomenons in his body. But about one thing he is sure that all these are happening without his control and efforts. But he is unable to stop or activate any of the functions of his body organs.

Due to the strong impact of *Maya* he associates his ego 'I' (*Ahankar*) with his physical body. As his information about the creation around him increases, his ignorance also increases tremendously. More and more questions daily arises to his mind, the answer of which he does not know.

It is a paradox that a young child has got only very few questions in his mind whose answer he does not know, but a learned old man has got millions of questions in his mind the answer of which he does not know. So we can rightly say that:

"To every new answer you can always ask at least two or more new questions. So although our information is expanding rapidly, but our ignorance is also expanding more rapidly."

As the knowledge of our Science & Technology is progressing, we are exposed with more & more mysteries of the wonderful universe, about living, non-living and heavenly bodies around us. Now we have billions of questions about the unexplained known & un-known mysteries, the answer of which we do not know. We are not leading from un-known to known, but form:

Un-known → known → more unknown → more Ignorence

Unknown (Our ignorance) + further scientific research → leads us to *more known information* → *but more known information leads us to more unknown questions and ignorance the answers of which we do not know* → *In this way we never lead to complete known Knowledge, but our ignorance is continuously increasing*

As per the *Taitiriya Upanishad,* the great *Rishi Bhirgu* aspired to know the ultimate reality. His father god *Varuna* advised him *"Tapas Brahma"* (Meditate on Brahma). After prolonged practice, Bhirgu realized that the entire existence came out of a *single universal matter (ether)*, in matter they abide and in matter they dissolve. But his father Varuna did not approved it and advised him to go ahead.

But after some time Bhirgu realized that everything in the universe has come out of the *vital-energy*, sustained by it and again dissolved into it. His father further advised him to go ahead and meditate more. Later Bhirgu realized that the ultimate reality is the *absolute wisdom*. But after meditating further he found that the ultimate reality is *Ananda* (infinite Joy and Bliss). In the last Bhirgu further realized that the ultimate truth is unfathomable silence and peace beyond description (Brahman).

We observe that the ultimate truth depends upon the level and state of our mind and consciousness. We may come to different conclusions depending on our mind. The ultimate truth is revealed only when the mind is peaceful and dissolves in *Brahman*, since mind is the biggest weapon Maya and works under its influence. Maya gets away only if mind is dissolved.

Remember: Knowledge does not mean information. Our known area of knowledge always remains finite and limited but the unknown area of knowledge is tremendously increasing day by day. Is there any way through by which our ignorance is totally removed forever and we can know the absolute truth?

It is strange that all the Fundamental Atomic & Subatomic Particles are Exactly Alike

A child learns in his school that matter is made up of atoms & molecules and further these are made up of subatomic particles like electron, proton, neutron and so many other elementary particles. But do we know every thing about these particles? Do we know what are their colors, shapes and sizes? By which material, the particles are made up of? Shall we ever be able to see and understand completely the subatomic particles? Till now we don't?

Is it not miraculous that the trillions of sub-atomic particles are exactly same and alike individually, throughout the vast universe?

For example: why all the electrons are exactly same in size, color, charge, mass and all other properties? There is no difference at all between any two electrons throughout the universe. Why are there no different types of electrons manufactured by nature? It means all the electrons and other sub-atomic particles had been created and controlled by one individual throughout the universe under the exact mathematical laws. It is a limitation of science that it can never make any two things exactly alike in all respect.

Universe is made from One Material

It is a common delusion of the mind that the universe has been made up from billions of different kind of materials and things. But according to science the matter can be converted into energy and the energy can be converted in to matter. All the atomic and sub-atomic particles are inter-convertible by nuclear reaction. This shows the equivalence between matter and energy. The great scientist Albert Einstein has given the famous formula $E=mc^2$. Where E is the energy created, m is the mass of the matter disappeared and c is the velocity of light. The energy produced by any different kind of atom is of the same kind not different. Why?

This equation proves that the matter and energy are the different physical forms of the same thing (God). It is just like that the ice, water and steam are the different form of same thing i.e. H_2O at different temperatures. All the fundamental particles consist the same material inside them.

Ice, water and steam appear to be different due to delusion. Science & Technology can now say with a great confidence that the whole universe including the *ether,* space, dark matter and dark energies are made up of only one kind of material. But they don't know exactly what this material is? The known visible material or energy is suspended in dark unknown matter. Visible matter is only 4%, dark matter is 23% and dark energies are 73% of the total matter in the universe.

How much do we know about it? From where, all these materials came from? What are its properties? Was it present before the creation or not? Who decided to create such atomic and sub-atomic particles? Who is the great Architect and who designed this wonderful universe, which provides us all kind of comforts, without expecting anything in return from us? Who created all the laws of sciences, before the creation started?

How Much We Know About Something

It is a common paradox that we say that we know most of the things. In fact we know only a little bit or just nothing about any thing. To illustrate my point, I would like to tell you the following interesting talk between a saint and his disciple. Once there was an interaction between a saint and his disciple as follows: -

Disciple: Guru Ji, what is God? How can I see God?

Saint: Have you seen India?
Disciple: Yes. I live in India and have seen it
Saint: Have you really seen the whole of India?
Disciple: No Guru Ji, I have seen only few cities.
Saint: Have you seen Delhi?
Disciple: Yes. I live in Delhi.
Saint: Have you seen each and every part of Delhi?
Disciple: No Guru Ji. I have seen only a few places in it.
Saint: Have you seen your house in Delhi?
Disciple: Yes. Naturally, I live in it.
Saint: Have you really seen every part of your house and
            its household goods etc?
Disciple: No. I have not seen everything in my house.
            There are still some places in my house, which I
            have never seen. I do not know all the things in
            my house.
Saint: Have you seen your own body?
Disciple: Yes. I daily see my body?
Saint: Your body is made up of billions of living cells.
            But have you ever seen all those cells of your
            body?
Disciple: No. I have not seen the cells of my body. They.
            are very small. I have heard that there are billions
            of cells in our body.
Saint: Have you seen the structure of all the body cells?
Disciple: No, I have heard that body cells have beautiful
            structure and can be seen though a powerful
            microscope.
Saint: Have you seen all the components of cell in your
            body? What chemicals are contained in the cells?
            How does they multiply each other? Do you
            know about the functioning of your sense organs,
            nerves, brain, mind, heart, kidneys and stomach
            etc. in your body?

Disciple: No, Guru Ji, I do not know all these.

The saint smiled and explained: when you have not seen each and every part of an object, how can you say that you have seen the object completely? Also to see an object is totally different than to know an object. When there is ignorance about the subsets of a set, how can we say that we know the whole set?

In fact we have only a little spark of information or a little bit of knowledge about something in the universe. We do not know any of the physical things completely. Remember, it is not scientific to say that we know an object completely.

We are trying to know God, but it is something different from all the material and immaterial objects and our ownself also. The God is the totality of both the manifested universe including us, and the un-manifested remaining part of God. Unless and until we know everything about both, we cannot say we know God completely. *Nothing remains to know further, after knowing God or our ownself.*

The saint further explained: A tree consists of many different parts like its roots, stem, branches, leaves, flowers, fruits etc. We cannot say that a particular portion or a part of the tree is the tree. Similarly we cannot say that any part of our physical body is our ownself. The totality of all the parts of a tree arranged in a systematic organized manner (already designed by God) can be called a tree.

If someone knows little bit about the leaves of a tree and say that he knows the whole tree is neither scientific nor logical. To know a tree we have to perceive it as a whole and also every particle inside it, all at a time and not in parts. Similarly to know God we have to perceive God as a whole

& every part of it, all at a time and not in parts at different times.

Wonderful Arrangement of Atomic and Subatomic Particles in Living & Non-living Beings

Till now our scientists have failed to actually see the atoms, molecules, electrons, protons, neutrons, photons etc. through any powerful microscope. We are unable to see smaller then a virus at present. What is the proof that all these particles exist? What are their shapes, colors, materials etc.? Why do you believe on these? Why do you all accept their existence without any proof? Has any body asked for their exact mathematical proofs? We all accept their existence, as it explains further in the development of all our scientific theories.

It is strange, why we all need the proof of God, who has hidden himself behind the whole creation? Can any phenomenon be explained ultimately without the acceptance of existence of God? Absolutely not. On the other side, the acceptance of God explains everything, where science fails to explain.

Atoms and molecules in living or non-living matter are not scattered in a haphazard random manner without any order, but are systematically arranged in a beautiful & well-defined network, which needs infinite intelligence to arrange. The arrangement of electrons, protons and neutrons in atoms of the same element anywhere in the universe is always exactly same.

Further the atoms & molecules are arranged beautifully, in elements, compound and crystals. The molecules of water (H_2O) and other fluids are always arranged in their solid, liquid or gaseous forms. There is not even a slightest amount of matter which is not arranged, any where in the universe, to give it a proper form & shape.

The complex molecules are further, beautifully & systematically arranged in living cells, body cells, viruses or bacterias. The arrangement of molecules in all the viruses or bacterias of the same kind is further exactly same. How the arrangement of billions of atoms and molecules in a cell, virus or bacteria can be done exactly same without the infinite intelligence (of God)? Science has to accept the existence of God for these arrangements. Who is arranging all the particles and giving them definite shapes? What is His aim?

Microcosmic View of Arrangement of Particles: Due to the great delusion or Maya, man is unable to see, through his naked eyes the arrangement and motion of the atomic and subatomic particles inside the matter around him. If he could see the matter through a powerful microscope he will find the atomic and subatomic particles are spinning in circular motion and also vibrating. No particle is at rest in the universe.

His naked eyes are unable to see the actual shape, motion, color and arrangement of the particles. The objects visible through a powerful microscope are entirely different than what the man sees with his naked eye. The naked eyes see the objects in the shape, as Almighty God wants man to see due to his delusion or *Maya*.

All the atoms or molecules of one substance are exactly alike in all respect all over the universe. There is no difference between any two molecules of the same substance anywhere. If we mix a drop of water into sea, it is impossible to search out and collect the same original molecules of the drop of water again by any scientific method or procedure, because all the molecules are alike and indistinguishable.

Further the microscopic living body cells, bacterias and viruses etc are made up of billions of atoms, complex molecules like RNA & DNA, chemicals, genes and other things all arranged in a beautiful organized manner. All living bodies are made up of by the complex arrangement of billions of living cells of different kinds. All these arrangements can't be done by the inert nature itself without infinite intelligence to organize.

Blood cells are constantly doing their great work of supplying the oxygen and heat energy to different parts of our body, which we are unable to know and control. Similarly in living plants and trees: water, fertilizers, chemicals and so many other things are constantly supplied from its roots to different parts of its body, not visible to our eyes. So all the microscopic particles are doing a huge amount of work continuously day and night without any break or rest, and without any knowledge of our mind to keep the world alive.

In fact God is doing all these works secretly, without men's knowledge and control. Due to delusion man is unable to see the actual shape of non-living matter & living beings. Whatever visible is exactly what the God wishes us to see? Without delusion or Maya the universe and world have been observed differently.

It is the will of God that He wants everybody to see the world in the manner He likes i.e. as it looks. If God stop the motion and arrangement of atomic particles even for a second there would have been no life at all.

Macroscopic View of Arrangement of Heavenly Bodies:
Our naked eyes are able to see only the moon, planets, Sun, few thousand stars, Milky- way, few galaxies and a few other heavenly bodies. But now with the help of a powerful telescope like Hubble Telescope, we are able to see more and more mysterious heavenly bodies like neutron stars, red-giant stars, black holes, quasars and billions of stars and galaxies in the universe. So whatever is visible through the naked eyes is not a reality, but a misleading delusion.

Our common sense interpret or misinterpret that the thousands of small tiny bright stars are suspended in the sky mysteriously and they do not fall on earth like other worldly objects. Star looks to naked eyes a few kilometers away. The sun, moon, planets and stars seem to revolve around the earth in a day and the earth seems to be at rest and also seems to be the centre of the universe. The earth looks flat. But we know that whatever the common sense interpret is not true. This is due to the delusion and *Maya*. Whatever the common sense interprets to our mind is exactly the same God wants us to observe, through His great delusion and keeps our mind away from the reality.

Question arises: can we ever know the reality? Yes, to know the absolute reality, God has given us the power of intelligence, through which we are able to remove our delusions. Science, technology and education are outcomes of human intelligence and exposing the recent new discoveries of heavenly bodies and the new structure of our universe.

The model of universe designed by our scientists is totally different than the model of the universe in the mind of an ordinary man, a child, a newly born baby, an animal, an insect and other living beings. But truth is always one and same, it cannot be many. If the universe is real it can't be interpreted by different beings in different manner. The universe should have been looked the same by every body at all times.

But due to the delusion of God it looks different to different individuals and creatures. God is controlling the minds of all the living beings. The concept of the universe is exactly the same in the mind of any living being, which the Almighty God wants it for him.

Our different interpretations of the universe are exactly like the different interpretations of an elephant's shape given differently by few totally blind men by birth. Similarly no man can tell the structure of the universe correctly with the help of ordinary human mind.

Concept of Universe is Different
in Different Minds of Living Beings

If an object or the universe looks differently to different individuals it can't be real. The universe visible to us is simply a concept in our mind, which differ from person to person. It differs even among the different scientists, since they are also under the same delusion as we are.

But the self-realized yogis (spiritual scientists) who have a victory over the great delusion and Maya of God have told us differently. According to them the universe is just a great dream or a condensed thought in the mind of God. All of us are simply images and the actors of a film in the world, (it is just like on the screen of a T.V. or cinema projected by a universal hidden projector.

We also know that the concept of universe is also not same to an individual at his different state of mind. When a man goes to a dream-sleep or a deep-sleep, he completely forgets even the existence of the awaken physical-universe. During sleep man is not even aware of his physical body and he does not care and bother for it. His body remains idle and lies in the physical universe unattended by him.

During dream mind of man is tuned to different cosmic viberation and creates a dream-universe, which is different from the physical-universe. The human brain is just like a T.V. tuner. It catches different receptions like different T.V. channels are cached when tuned differently

During dream man creates an astral body for him to act, which is not made up of physical matter. He has no control over dreams during his sleep. He generally forgets the relationships with his acquaintances. His dreams are generally totally irrational and illogical too.

Generally when we see in dream our near & dear ones who are already dead, we forget that they are already dead. Some times an old man dreams that he is a child. He forgets his past history & experiences that he is not a child but an old grown up man.

It is wrong to say that these dreams are the exact manifestation and repetition of our past memories, stored in our mind just like computer memories stored in a hard disc are retrieved. If it had been the repetition of the past memories, it would have been rational & just the same replica of the past memories. But it is not so.

About Sleep Dreams and Death

When we go to sleep we have to detach our mind completely from every thing of the physical awakened world. We have to completely forget our body and leave it unattended for some time by us in this world. Even a single thought of attachment to this world will be a hindrance to go to sleep state.

After enjoying dream or sleep for some time we come back again in the awakened world. What is the purpose of these dreams? By these dreams and sleep daily Almighty God is trying His best to realize us that we are under delusion and the physical universe is not a reality. But we are ignoring his efforts due to Maya.

The particular dream, which we are going to experience tonight, can never be predicted. The dreams are irrational and illogical in nature and have negligible relationship with our physical world. Generally the dreams are such, which we have never thought of in advance. Some times the dreams may give us glimpses of our past lives and some times of our future life too. But the dreams may or may not be true. We know that a dream is unreal.

Similarly a dream universe is either the creation of our own mind or it is a thought in the mind of God. God has also created the physical universe in His mind as a thought. But it is certain that we are helpless to experience dream as per the choice of God and cannot dream as per our own choice or will. We are forced to experience pain & pleasure, laugh & weep, fear & joy, falling from a height, excitements, our own death and accidents etc. as per the fruits of our past actions or *karmas*.

Any Desire at Death is the Cause of Rebirth

At the time of our death, we have to leave every thing permanently in this world included our physical body. But if we have any desire or attachment to anything in this world at the time of death we will come back to this world again to fulfill our desires. Death is not instantly, but it takes some time by the soul to leave the body. At the time of death our sensations in different parts of the body is lost one by one slowly. Sense organs are lost one by one as during meditation. The hearing sensation remains in a dead body for quite a long time after death.

After our death our soul is given another ethereal or astral body for some time to act, just like we get a body in our dreams. This body possesses sense organs, brain, mind, intelligence etc. We live in this body, in an astral universe that is obtained by tuning our mind to a different cosmic frequency, till we find a suitable womb to take birth again in this world.

But if we don't have any attachment and desire at the time of death, and have a strong desire to merge in God or to know God, we get *Moksha* after death. Moksha means no births or rebirths and merge in God forever, like a water bubble merge in sea.

When we are awakened after the sleep, we are astonished to find ourselves in this awakened world. We analyze that dream world is not real and we were under a great delusion and *Maya* during sleep. But it is again due to the influence of *Maya* on our mind that we do not analyze that the physical world too is under *Maya* just like the dream universe. Our mind is like a TV tuner, tuned to different channels.

Our universe is not a reality. The whole universe has been projected in the great mind of God. It is just like a universal four-dimension projector projects on a 4-dimensional space-time screen. Whatever is visible or happening in the universe is not real but false images. We can realize the truth of this if we go out of the delusion and *Maya*.

The deep sleep state of mind is different from dream sleep state. In deep sleep our mind is tuned to different cosmic frequency, where there is nothing to interact, no time, no place, no space and nothing else etc. After enjoying deep sleep we report that there was nothing in the deep sleep. But we cannot say that we were not there in existence during deep sleep state and time is passed quickly. We are the observer, a witness and have experienced the deep sleep. It means where there was nothing in deep sleep, we must be present there in that nothing as a witness to observe it.

In the deep sleep state we are very near to God and very near to our own true self 'I'. Instead of sleep, if we could go to this deep sleep with an awakened consciousness, we are under meditation and can know our own self. Through the experience of deep sleep God is showing us a path to know our own self.

The universe appears to us exactly what Almighty God wants us to see. We all are His children. *God never takes rest and never go to sleep even for a second.* Out of His divine love, He is constantly taking care of all of his children without any break or rest. But due to His infinite love and kindness, He daily provides us sleep, to recharge our tired body with life force, and also gives us the actual experience of the non-reality of the physical universe.

Our scientists are **not exceptions** to this power of delusion and *Maya* of God. They are as much under the delusion and *Maya* as we are. Therefore the scientists will not be able to know the absolute reality of the creator and his creation, unless they remove their own ignorance due to delusion and *Maya* as advised by so many self-realized saints, who have realized God. As for any scientific experiment a well-equipped lab, a thorough knowledge of the experiment and the guidance of the learned scientists are required, similarly for a spiritual experiment, the yogic scientists require the purification of body, mind and sprit. No scientist can enter the kingdom of God unless he strictly follows the path of spirituality as advised by scriptures. It is unjustifiable and unscientific to declare the non-existence of God, without any proper experimentation.

If the sea-divers do not go into deep bed of sea, they may not get even a single pearl from sea. How can they declare that there are no pearls in the sea without reaching and searching the seabed?

This can be explained through the **story of a frog inside a well**, which had never gone out of the well in his life. For the frog the well is the whole universe and nothing is outside the well. But if anyhow the frog gets a chance to come out of the well his concept of the universe is totally changed.

Similarly our universe is like a cosmic dark well or an ocean of ignorance (*andhakoop*). We (including our scientists) can never go out of this *andhakoop*, till we get self-realization.

Till we are in the *andhakoop* we are under *Maya* therefore we can never understand the reality of the creator (God) and the creation (universe). Our *Shastras* has given us the scientific yogic methods to go out of the *andhakoop* and to know God.

The Great Dreamer of The Future
Nostradamus

Nostradamus was a physician of France born in 1555 A.D. He is the finest example of a miraculous man who dreamed about the important world events of the future world. He had predicted many thousand great events of the world out of which nearly half of the predictions had come out to be true. The rest of the events will occur in the next few hundred years or so.

There had been so many saints in the world who had the ability of most accurate predictions. There are so many genius astrologers in India and other countries who are able to predict accurately on the basis of astrological mathematical calculations. There are so many ordinary persons whose dreams come out to be true so many times.

As per mathematical and scientific logic *even if one such prediction has ever came out to be true* in the history of earth, it is a sufficient proof that the events or the dream drama of the universe is pre-planned and a program already stored in the mind of God. All the events in the universe are happening in a systematic pre-planned manner, except the man has been given a little freedom to act to some extant.

Our universe is not just a *random accidental happening* or creation by chance, out of nothing and without any purpose. But it is well planned, fully programmed and well organized. It is beautifully arranged and has a great purpose behind the creation. The human life is also not just purposeless, fruitless and aimless as said by some ignorant authors. The Creator has a purpose to send us on this earth. **What is that purpose? Try to find it out.** Is it not true that we are terribly busy with the studying of the creation only and ignoring the study of the creator intentionally?

The Universe is Not Eternal, It took Birth and will Vanish at the End

It is now almost certain with a great accuracy that the age of the universe is between 12 to 20 billion years. Hubble Telescope has verified it. It means that our universe did not exist before 20 billion years ago. It has taken a birth long ago, and before that there was no time, no stars, no heavenly bodies, no earth, no water, no air, no fire, no space, no *ether*, no matter, no energy, no fields, no rays, no particles, no human beings and none of the living creatures. It leads to so many eternal **un-answered questions** before the humanity, which are to be unsolved?

It is logical & acceptable by all the scientists that *there can't be any creation without any creator.* To every effect there must be a cause. **Cause & Effect Law** must hold. Here arises a big question: Was there only one thing or so many things or nothing before the creation of the universe? It is logical and mathematical that if there was nothing before the creation, then the universe can't be created, of its own, out of nothing or without any cause? There must be some body, which has created the mysterious universe.

Science has observed that not even a single particle can be created out of nothing nor destroyed to nothing in the universe. Matter & Energy are inter-convertible. These can be changed into one form to another. Not even a single atom or a particle can be created or destroy of its own. Science has also observed that the universe has been made up of only one material and not two or more materials. The whole universe is made up of the same kind of visible matter throughout, which obeys the same laws of Natural Sciences, everywhere. The visible matter and energies have come out of dark matter and dark energies, still unknown to us.

How wonderful it is that the same laws of Natural Science are applicable in this vast Universe having a diameter approx. 20 billion light years. No scientific laws of natural sciences can be created of its own. Scientists are busy only to search or to find out the laws, which already exist in the *ether* since the beginning. So there must be a creator of all the laws of natural sciences, which we have searched through our scientific & technological researches. The scientists are further puzzled with great questions like:

❑   Who created the universe?
❑   Why the universe was created? What is the purpose behind the creation?
❑   For whom it was created, when there was none other?
❑   What material was used to create universe, as there was no material available before creation? How the heavenly bodies, matter, atomic and sub-atomic particles and living beings came into existence?
❑   How the non-materials like Ego, Mind, Intelligence, Pain, Pleasure, Sorrow, Bliss, Joy, Sex, Senses, Prana (Life Energy) and other Cosmic Energies came into existence?
❑   When was the beginning of time?
❑   Can the time run backward i.e. from future to past?

❑   Is the universe finite or infinite or does it have any boundary or limits? What is beyond the universe?

❑   What are dark matter and dark energies?

Due to the strong impact of *Maya* and delusion our scientists are unable to answer these questions correctly.

It is well known that the Natural Sciences can provide answer of only **how** of a phenomenon or an event happened but cannot answer satisfactorily the **why** of a phenomenon or an event have happened. The questions mentioned above are beyond the preview of the Natural Sciences. But the explanation to these questions has already been given in our *Shastras & the Vedas*, which are the oldest in the world. This clearly proves that our ancestors were much more intelligent and spiritually advanced.

Brahman is the Only Reality

Brahman is the name for the ultimate, unchanging, reality, composed of pure being and consciousness. *Brahman* lies behind the apparent multiplicity of the phenomenon world, and is ultimately identical to the *Atman* or inner essence of the human being. *Vedas* have clearly declared *"Braham vidam brahamaive bhavati* (the knower of Brahman becomes Brahman).

Vedas affirms that before the creation of the universe there was only one thing i.e. *Brahman (God alone)*. He was in His absolute state of rest, *i.e. Sat, Chit and Ananda* (Truth-Consciousness-Eternal Bliss). There was no other individual and no material or immaterial thing to share his infinite powers like Omnipotence, Omniscience, Omnipresent, Infinite Intelligence, Mind and Love etc. All His infinite powers were lying idle, because none else was present.

As sugar cannot taste sugar itself, some one else is needed to taste sugar. One cannot love oneself; someone else is needed to love. Similarly God also needs some one else to enjoy and experience his Super Powers and Supreme-Love. So He decided to create the universe from Himself and for Himself. He also created *Maya* or ignorance to divide and separate the creation from Him and also created so many individual souls.

There was no other body, material, energy or field except God alone. So through His delusion & *Maya,* He decided to transform Himself into different kind of living beings, space, ether, air, fire, water, materials and heavenly bodies. All the different kind of matter and energies are nothing but God Himself. Since there was none other, He created the universe for Himself, by Himself and for none else.

So it is self evident that the He Himself is the whole universe both manifested and unmanifested. **Whole Universe is God's Physical Body**, made up of Himself and for Himself alone. He has a full control on each and every atom of the universe. It is strange that we human beings have either no control or a very little control on our physical body.

Due to delusion we don't know even different parts and organs inside our body and how the are functioning inside our body? What chemical actions and reactions are always going on in our body? We can't change our body system as per our own sweet will, choice or desire.

All the atomic and sub-atomic particles are the **manifestation of 'Shiva & Shakti'**. *Shakti* means power or energy. *Shakti* is the manifestation of Goddess *Mahakali* or

Durga (wife of Lord Shiva). We know that the centre of each atom known as the nucleus is stationary, which contains protons & neutrons. The electrons revolve & whirl around its nucleus with a very high speed.

Is it not miraculous & strange that all the particles like electron, proton & neutrons spin billions of times in a second around their axis? Also the electrons revolve billion times in a second around their nucleus. It is strange that inspite of such a large number of revolutions inside the atom none of the particle collide with each other.

The nature without an infinite intelligence and control can't do it. This can only be possible by accepting the infinite intelligence and planning of God working behind the nature. Only God can do it. The nucleus of each atom is relatively stationary is nothing but *'Lord Shiva'* and the electron revolving round the nucleus (*Shiva*) is nothing but Goddess *'Shakti'*. Therefore all the atoms in the universe are nothing but a divine sort of manifestation of *'Shiva & Shakti'*. Lord *Shiva* is sitting at the centre of each atom and the Goddess *Shakti* is revolving round *Shiva*.

Microscopically due to great impact of delusion and *Maya*, human beings are unable to see actual motion of the atomic and sub-atomic particles and the reality. Due to delusion we see only what the almighty God desires and wants us to see. The human mind is under the direct control of the Super Mind of God.

On the other hand the microscopic structure of a living body is also a well-organized arrangement of billions of microscopic living organism known as cell. Further these cells in a living body are not randomly or haphazardly placed but are beautifully arranged in an organized network.

As the blood cells are constantly moving and doing the great work of supplying oxygen, heat and so many chemicals to different parts of the body.

Similarly in plants and other living bodies water, food, minerals & chemicals are supplied to different parts by living cells. All these microscopic fine works are not visible to human naked eyes due to the great delusion and *Maya*.

If the human eyes were able to see the motion of these tiny particles and the living cells, the world would have been looked quite different to us and not as beautiful and attractive as it is now. It is the great **Will** of God Father that we see the world as He wants us to see.

Macroscopically: Human eyes are unable to see and observe the whole universe all at a time. The human eyes can look only a tiniest and negligible portion of the universe at a time. We can never see the whole Sun or the whole Earth at a time. But God can see not only the whole universe but also each and every atomic and subatomic particle all at a time and forever. Every thing is under His full control.

Each Galaxy consists of billions of stars like Sun and each star has so many planets revolving around it. There are billions of such galaxies in the universe. Each galaxy has thousands of Black Holes, Novas, Super Novas, Neutron Stars, Red-giant stars and Quasars etc. There may be so many other mysterious heavenly bodies about which science does not know even today.

A Neutron Star is
Condensed Form of Dieing Matter

A Neutron star has a very small size of few meters only, but has a huge mass and huge gravitation. Its mass may be much more then our Sun and the gravitation on its surface is millions time more than the Sun. The matter inside this is in the neutron state of matter. In a neutron state of matter the space inside and outside the atomic & sub-atomic particles is minimized. In this state the whole galaxy may be reduced to a size of few kilometers and our earth will reduce to a size less then a football. It is a scientific law that any thing that takes birth in the universe must die one day. Nothing is immortal except God. The matter inside the Neutron Star is in its dieing state and finally to be digested by God.

Black Holes are the Mouth of God
to Digest the Creation

A Black hole is a huge dead star in neutron state of matter, but it has much more mass and gravitation than a neutron star. The gravitation on its surface is so huge that nothing can escape out from its surface. While radiations can escape from a neutron star, but none can escape from Black Hole. Any radiation including light again falls back into it due to huge gravitation. So nothing can come out of it and we cannot get any information of the object, which have once fallen into the black whole. Such an object simply stops existing for us forever.

You will wonder if by chance any object or a star comes under its gravitation, it will fall into it and we can never know any thing further about it. It is also strange that a Black Hole becomes more powerful after it digests a star or a galaxy. These black wholes are nothing but the **Mouths of**

God through which the Almighty God is digesting and annihilating its creation. This is the role of Lord Shiva, who is the Lord of destruction.

In one portion of the universe new stars and new galaxies are created, in another portion so many stars and galaxies are disappearing through these black wholes. This creation and annihilation of heavenly bodies can never be without the Super Powers of God. (Bhagwad Geeta Chapter XIII).

**Newly Discovered
Dark Matter & Dark Energies**

As per the report of Hindustan Times dated 20th December 2003, the Cosmologists have now found evidences through the space researches that the universe mainly consists of mysterious new things called *'dark matter' and 'dark energies'*. The ordinary visible matter is only about 4% about which we know only a very little. The invisible Dark matter is 23%. The remainder 73% matter is dark energies. Till now the scientists do not know any thing about these dark matter & dark energies.

Scientists say that Universe is expanding & the galaxies are pulled apart due to these dark energies and also pushed together by gravitational energy. It appears that the great force of repulsion due to dark matter and great force of attraction due to gravity are opposite and reactive forces to each other. In my opinion dark matter is nothing but *ether* present through out the universe and the dark energies are nothing but all the hidden energies like Life-energy, Cosmic energy & Kundalini energy etc. of God. Scriptures and yogis already know these things. All the visible matter, dark matter and dark energies have come out of Anahat Sound of

Om. These three unitedly are the constituents of the *Akash Tatva* (Space). Om is the first manifestation of Brahman.

A computer is one of the greatest gifts to man from God. But most of the non-believers think that one-day man will be able to manufacture a man from robot in the factories. This is a great misconception that they think that a computer has got an ego 'I', infinite intelligence and feelings too. In fact they do not know that a computer · has got zero intelligence, no feelings and no ego.

A computer simply computes very fast. It has no mind, no intelligence and no soul. It can never differentiate between beautiful and ugly, or good & bad. It can never have feelings of worries, happiness & sorrows, pains & pleasures, sleep & dream, joy & bliss, and laugh & weep etc. A computer is only a 100% obedient idiot servant but computes very fast.

We will never be able to create, any living being, without taking anything or something originally as the basic cause of life already existed & created by God.

A little knowledge is a dangerous virus in our brain. It creates a false pride in us, kills our curiosity to know further, due to the influence of Maya. We should never be satisfied with our little learning and knowing of new things. We should never be proud of our vast learning and knowledge. More we know about known or unknown, more we come to know about the unknown. Known is always limited & finite, but the unknown always remains infinite and increases too.

If you could feel once even a spark of divine love, so great would be your joy & bliss...overpowering you ...that you will hanker after Him for the rest of your life. That is why the name of God is Hari (who deprives you of all worldly attachments).

The greatest romance one can have is the romance with God...God is the Supreme-Lover and our souls are His beloved. During deep meditation, when our soul meets the greatest Lover of the universe, then the eternal divine romance begins, which gives us joy & bliss. It is different from sex, which is an animal instinct.

We must have clear understanding and a strong will power to control our mental emotions, discrimination between right & wrong, or good & bad actions. Only our right & pure thoughts and feelings can bring us the greatest happiness and joy in life.

Om Peace, Peace, Peace

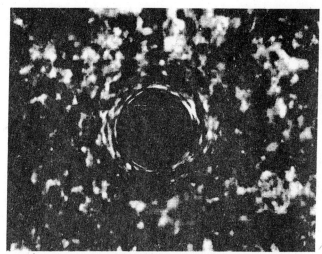

See the rare picture of a **black hole***. Gravity inside is
so huge that not even vibrations can escape out of it.

A **Galaxy*** is collection of billions of stars like Sun & span nearly
10,000 light years. There are billions of such Galaxies in the
universe.

---

* Curtsy from NASA. Pictures taken by Hubble Space Telescope.

3

The Nature of Our Dreams and Death

3
The Nature of our Dreams & Death

Prayer

O Director of Dream Worlds! O Creator of thoughts and the Lord of Dream-Universe! Teach me to understand Thy great mystery of my sweet and horrible dreams. Teach me to understand Thy great Dream-Movie of the wondrous universe around me. How my thoughts, past memories and future events are combined and converted into dreams during my sleep? How to interpret the dreams we experience? Since my birth, I am not only curious to know Thy creation, but also curious to know my mysterious dreams.

I am forced to experience unwillingly the horrible dreams during my sleep just as a puppet. Virtually I do not have any control over my dreams and I experience helplessly the horrible, fearful & unreasonable dreams. My little mind is not able to understand their cause, meaning and the purpose behind them.

I am standing on the brink of eternity, ready to jump from the world of delusion into Thee. Make me to realize my oneness with Thee. Awaken me permanently from my false awakened dream of Thy delusive universe, so that I am able to remember Thee forever. The nightmare of death, rebirth and delusion always dances around me. I do not know what happens at the time of death and after death? How my soul takes rebirth again and again? Do humans take rebirth as lower creatures also?

O, Beloved One, O Spirit Divine, Thou have created the *Satan* (*Maya*) to separate us from Thee. Let the *Satan* may not delude those who are seeking Thee. The *Satan* is very strong and powerful, but Thy love is far greater and potent. One touch of Thy grace and love can drive away the *Satan* controlling my mind, intelligence, senses, heart, body and my fate.

O Father! I don't want anything except Thee. I can't live without Thee. I don't want to teach anyone, but discipline my ownself. What is there in anything, O Lord of dreams?

I am convinced that everything in this world is false and a dream. Even my body is a dream in the awakened world. My desires are also dreams. Thou art the only reality behind this dream-drama world. Make me free from this delusive dream of *Maya*. O, Eternal Omniscient Light, awake me from the dark dream world, and take me to the Eternal Ocean of Thy Infinite Light.

What are Dreams

To understand our ego 'I' first we have to understand about the mystery of our dreams. All of us are experiencing the dreams helplessly, during our sleep and we have no control of our mind on our dreams. During the sleep state of consciousness, our physical body lies uncared and unbothered by ourself. During sleep state we are not aware of our physical body at all and also not aware of any thing of this universe

The universe, which exists during our awakening state, does not exist during our sleep or dream state of consciousness. The dream universe is a creation of our mind and is different from the awakened-universe. Our mind is like a *TV tuner* and is tuned to different cosmic frequency of dream world, during our sleep. During awakening the frequency of tuning is different. This should be clearly understood that *"no dream can come to us without any cause behind it"*. The cause may be anything, even the fruits of our past *karmas*. But can we predict by any scientific way about the dream we are going to experience in the following night? Is it possible?

The **thought-films** of all our past experiences of this life and previous lives are stored in the memory of our mind. It is like the storage of memory in the hard disk of a computer. *The dreams are the mental motion pictures projected by our unconscious mind. The dreams are the creation of God and not always purposeless as generally thought. Dreams have a great purpose of God to realize men about the dream nature of this false world.* The creation of the dreams for man is to provide the proof that this universe, which looks real, is false and is also like a dream.

We create and possess a *subtle body (made from ethereal matter and* not from physical matter) for ourself during the dream world and we have a power to create a new dream universe for us. The subtle body possesses all the five sense organs, five organs for actions, mind, intelligence and ego 'I' etc. During our dream we are forced to experience all kinds of emotions like joy, pleasures, happiness and grief, sorrows and pains, fear, laugh and weeping etc. We may also experience our death.

Generally when we see our dead relations during our dreams we forget that they are already dead. Some times the old man experiences that he is a young child and forgets all his past history. How it is all? It appears that nothing is in our hands during our dreams. Our helplessness of experiencing the dream which are not of our own choice clearly proves that we aré just puppet in the hands of Almighty God in the Dream-Drama of the world.

Dreams are the Materialization of Thoughts

All the ancient *Shastras* are the creation of God. They are universally true forever. It is a misconception that *Shastras* are exclusively for Hindus. Before three millenniums or Christ there was hardly any other religion except Sanatan Dharma in the world.

There are evidences of human skulls nearly seven million years old found in Botswana, South Africa (A News in H.T. dated 12-7-2002). This discovery has shaken and challenged all the previous baseless imaginary concepts and theories of historians and scientists. It further confirms the authenticity of the *Vedas,* Hindu *Shastras* and *Puranas.* Will the historians tell us the human history of this last seven million years?

In fact the *Shastras* and the *Puranas* are for whole humanity belonging to the people of all the religions. All human beings have equal right on the *Shastras* created by God for the benefit of all the men. The *Shastras* have explained that our universe is a materialization of the great *Thought of God and it is a Cosmic Dream of God.* This may be little difficult for us to realize, to understand and to accept the truth in it.

Our dreams are the materialization of our thoughts in combination with our stored memories and the fruits of past actions of the present and previous lives. It is true that some times the dreams give the glimpses of our past & future. Thoughts are invisible, but can be made visible as dreams by the cosmic life energy as invisible steam can be condensed to visible water. When thoughts are further condensed and materialized they take the form of dream, like the water vapors when condensed change into liquid. When dream is further condensed it takes the form of material things as the liquid water when solidified changes into ice.

It can easily be understood by the example of making a film. First the invisible thoughts come in the mind of a director of a movie film. The invisible thoughts are further visualized or dreamed in the mind of the director in so many different ways. Then he further picturize or materialize his dream thought into a motion film through the acting by the actors. The motion film when played on a screen gives the illusion of reality to the viewers of the film

The viewers and observers of the movie film think that every thing shown on the screen is real. But a little logical thinking convinces the viewers that the film is a combination of series of millions of pictures fitted together and projected on a screen. The cosmic universe is merely a dream projected by God on the 4-dimensional space-time screen of the universe as told by the self-realized saints. The God's projector and His created films are far better then the man created ones. That is why the universe looks just real to us.

As per the Bhagwad Gita, we are the **immortal souls** and have taken birth on this earth to enjoy the fruits of our past actions (*karmas*) and to fulfill our unfulfilled desires We should see the entire happening around us, simply as an observer of three or four dimensional movie film, projected around us by God. Every thing around us is a false image and not the reality as our image in a plane mirror also looks like the real one. But remember our soul is immortal, unchangeable and unaffected by anything from this dream.

As we have the power to materialize our thoughts in dreams, God has the omnipotent power to materialize or dematerialize any of His thought in the universe. So a man when achieves self-realization becomes one with God, he attains all the powers of God. He can then materialize or dematerialize any thing at his will. Jesus Christ who was the 'Son of God', demonstrated this truth, so many times in his life by performing so many miracles. He was able to cure so many persons from incurable diseases and gave life to even dead persons.

It is rightly said that if you want to *know an atom completely*, you have to become atom yourself, if you want to *know Albert Einstein completely* you have to become Einstein yourself and if you want to *know God completely*, you have to become God yourself.

To Create or Materialize any Object
First a Thought is required

We know that everything on earth is, either man-made or God-made or made by some living creatures. It is universally accepted that nothing can be made without any cause. Whenever a thing is manufactured in a factory, first **a thought or an idea** comes in the mind of the engineer. And then the thought is visualized and materialized to manufacture the thing. There cannot be any thing without first having an idea or a thought about it.

Similarly whatever is in the universe or on the earth is not just by accident and it is not possible without any initial cause or a thought or an idea. There must be a cause for everything existing in the universe (Law of Cause & Effect). First the idea or thought of the universe came to the mind of God and then it was materialized into physical form in exactly the pre-decided design. A single thought was enough for God, to design the whole universe from the beginning till the end of the universe.

Remember as water (liquid) is a condensation of steam (gas), and ice (solid) is a condensation of water, similarly *dreams are condensation of thoughts and materials are the condensations of dreams.*

Various Illusions of Dreaming Man & Death

The dreams are generally seem to be **irrational, puzzling** and stray in nature and not much connected with our daily life experiences. During the dream the existence of our awakened universe is completely lost. We totally forget the existence of universe and the body we live in. If we are suffering with a sever pain and sorrow due to an accident before sleep, these are lost and forgotten during the dreams.

Reciprocally, someone may experience during a dream that he has murdered some one and for that he is going to be crucified soon. Little after he watches that he is crucified and has died also. After that, his horrible dream is broken and he is awakened from his dream. He is wondered to realize that his horrible dream was totally false imagination, and he is still alive. Nothing has happened to his body and it is safe. After this he has realized and convinced that it was all **illusion motion film** and he was forced to dream it.

Conversely he may experience the similar false nature of his real life universal dream in which he is living. One day he may meet a sudden accident and has broken most of his bones. Then he suffers with severe unbearable pain and suddenly he dies. But immediately he again *wakes up in an astral world* after his death. He may wonder to find that he has another *astral* body to act and experience. He may realize that he was dreaming in the false physical universe and has awakened in another astral universe.

He realizes that his present new astral body is perfectly O.K. His bones are also O.K. He is not dead, but still alive. He also wonders and finds some mysterious things that his new body does not feel hunger and need no food or water and so many other things to survive. He may laugh at his past dream of fetal accident in the awakened-world. This is what generally happens to most of the ordinary men at the time of death and after death. Has science done anything on these important topics?

What is Death and
Is Death a Dream

Birth and death are the two face of the same coin i.e. life. These are the two most important events through which everybody has to pass from one dream to another dream. Our lives, which look so real are just nightmares and dream pleasures. Death is simply a kind of dream matter, which sends us back into the consciousness of God or in some other astral worlds. Death releases the soul from the bondages of the physical body, and to precede the soul's journey back to God.

So d*eath is not a punishment* to us as it is generally presumed. But it is a *gift of God* and is a part of the process of salvation and *Moksha* of our soul. It is a fundamental law that whoever has taken birth has to die one day, even the inert matter, the universe, any literature or religion, if taken birth will vanish one day. But our soul is immortal and a spark of God. It was always there before our birth and will remain after our death. It will never die, but will merge with God again after salvation.

It is notable that only human beings have been given the right of salvation and self-realization of God. If the souls and even the deities want to free themselves from the pangs of births, deaths and the miseries of life, they have to take a birth in human form and seek God for salvation or *Moksha*. Only the human soul will merge in the Ocean of God.

Our reincarnations are a series of dreams within the great cosmic dream. When we daily see every body dieing and suffering at death, we feel that God is cruel to the world, by creating horrible death. In fact it is not so. *God is merciful even at our death.* Remember that the world is not real; it is a dream in the mind of God. God makes us free from the bondages of the world and gives us either salvation (*Mukti*) or another astral body after our death.

Our new astral body go to an astral world after our death, where we realize that we do not feel hunger, need no food, no fire can burn us, no water can drawn us, no need of any transport and so many necessities of life. In the astral world we are free from all kinds of bondages, diseases, troubles and fears due to the perishable physical body. But if some of desires had been left unfulfilled in our life, then after some time we would like to come back to earth to fulfill our unfulfilled desires. *So the unfulfilled desires are the cause of our rebirths.* If we have no desire and we remember God, at the time of death, then there will be no rebirth and we will merge in the Ocean of God forever.

The reincarnation of a soul can be in any part of the world. You may take birth in a country, which you hate and do not like. You may take birth in the family of your enemy or in the religion you do not like. You must have to account for all your past actions. Will you continue helplessly to take births and rebirths and experience all the horrible troubles of the delusive world? Or will you like to follow the path of salvation for no more births and rebirths? It depends entirely upon you.

If you identify your soul with your body or with the unreal world, you will be facing lots of troubles and sufferings. Our life is not real and we are under a great delusion due to *Maya*. The world is a Great Drama. Remember w*e are dreaming this world inside the Dream of God.* We are experiencing so many pleasure and sorrows in the dream delusion world.

The Universe is a Condensation and Materialization of the Dream of God

Whatever dream we experience, it must have a **cause**. Almighty God must have designed that dream for us. No dream can occur randomly, without any purpose and without any cause. In order to understand the process of materializing thoughts into dreams, we must be able to concentrate on our thoughts and by our strong will power, till they are converted into visible manifestations or dreams. This is known as visualization of thoughts i.e. thoughts are condensed into dreams. By learning further concentration on our dreams, we can learn to materialize dreams into material objects. The material objects around us are condensation of the dreams of God by the great will of God.

The yogis who achieve this power can materialize and dematerialize any object at their sweet will. Such yogis have already realized their unity with God as Jesus Christ.. By regular practice the yogis achieve the great power of concentration on thought and the power of visualization and they are able to demonstrate any miracle to their disciples.

I do not deny that there may be some cheaters, who may use some magical tricks to show a miracle to lure the innocent people. But it is unscientific and mischievous to conclude and declare that all the persons having the power of miracles are simply magicians and cheaters and nobody can perform any miracle.

Our pains and aches disappear from the screen of our consciousness during our sleep. If life was not a dream, you couldn't get away from your pains and aches even during the sleep or dream. We should look at this world as a great dream or a **movie film observer** and should not indulge into it.

We should not take everything in the film very seriously. In the world we may observe the great disparity like poor and rich, healthy and sick, pain and pleasure, powerful and weak etc. Still all living beings are playing their roles as assigned to them (by God) and enjoying the fruits of their past-karmas (actions). Take it as such. It is a truth.

Every thing is coming to us from a great factory of God. Don't you agree with this? To criticize God for everything wrong is most un-scientific. As per the plan of God, God is

not supposed to solve all the problems of the world, which
have been created by us.

To solve the problems of the world, God has given us the
power of discrimination and intelligence. If God is supposed
to solve all our problems, then the world drama will be no
more interesting for man. Our life will become dull and
purposeless like an animal life. But once we realize it fully
that the universe is a condensation of the dream of God, all
our desires and sufferings will vanish. We shall become
peaceful and calm. Realize it, it is possible.

Dream Nature of the World

The past experiences of the world have trained our mind in
so many different ways. Our mind is attuned with so many
baseless and needless desires. We have begun to think that
we couldn't be happy, if our desires are not fulfilled. This is
false. We should always try to make our life as simple as
possible by minimizing all our desires and needs. Otherwise
the bitter experiences of life will lead us to sorrows and
sufferings.

In our dream we may met with a fetal accident and
experience that we have lost our body limbs. But when we
wake up, we find everything O.K. We laugh and say, "Oh,
what a fool I am. It was only a false dream and not a
reality." It is exactly the same, during samadhi, when we
wake up in God; we realize the truth that the world is a
dream in God. We all are simply images in the dream of
God. Nothing is real in the world. Death is also a dream or
nightmare. We are only dreaming the suffering from death.

We should not be afraid of anything in the world, as it is all
a big dream. Nothing can harm our immortal soul the

observer of dream. The dreams created by God are not to harm us, but to educate and to realize us that there is no reality in the world. Even our death is also a dream and we are awakened in the astral world after our death with a new astral body to act.

Now we may be convinced intellectually that life is a dream thought of God, but it is not sufficient, unless we realize it completely. We all are already trapped in the great ocean of delusion due to Maya and it is our sad state of mind and consciousness. We must do our best efforts to escape this trap of Maya and try to realize God at the earliest in this life. Do not postpone your efforts, as we do not know when the death will come and which shall be our last breath to leave this temporary world?

Our love to enchanting world is perishable, but our love to God is more enchanting, pure, eternal and everlasting.

4
Spirit and Self-Realization

4

Spirit & Self-Realization

Prayer

O Heavenly Spirit! O Ocean of Knowledge! Thou art the dearest of the dear, nearest of the near, and the closest of the closest. Thou art just behind the curtain of our ignorance, vision and enchanting senses. Thou art the beauty of the flowers, forest, mountains and the miraculous beauty of the vast sky. Whenever, I look in my heart, Thou art inside.

Thou art the greatest Lover in universe and our souls are Thou beloved. As the worldly loves are not permanent, I am always crying for Thy Supreme Love, which is pure, loving and eternal. When Thou will have a mercy upon us and play a divine romance with Thy beloveds? Thou beloveds are waiting; to have a romance with Thee, since thousands of our past lives. Thou art also waiting for our love too but playing the game of hide & seek. O Lover of disciples! Now reveal Thee.

How to Get Self-Realization

For the seekers of God & self-realization, I may suggest a few holy books that are most useful as their holy Bibles, in their divine path of Yoga. Some of them are:

1.   **Bhagwad Geeta** (*The Song of the Lord & Bible of yogis*) is the most important sacred and authentic holy book for the seekers of God all over the world. This is the only Holy Book, in which the God Himself has opened Thy own

secrets. It is one of the greatest philosophical and yogic dialogues known to man.

Through Bhagwad Geeta, Lord Krishna has given the Knowledge of God in most condensed form and to the whole world through His dearest closest friend and disciple Arjuna. It is the Holy Bible for yogis and seekers of God. It is a guide for the inner path of self-realization.

All the *Puranas* also support the truth of Bhagwad Geeta. The *Puranas* are the records of great historical spiritual events with a great teaching motto and philosophy. But *Bhagwad Geeta* is a pure spiritual Knowledge and Truth about God revealed by Lord Krishna Himself for the benefit of the whole world through Arjuna. Knowledge is that which removes ignorance or *Maya* and brings us nearer to God. *Maya* keeps us away from God. Bhagwad Geeta informs us briefly what God is, and what are the different paths of seeking God?

Every one of us is full of anxieties and tensions, because of *Maya*. Our existence is in the atmosphere of non-existence. *Bhagwad Gita* is a search light for our intelligence in darkness to take the righteous decision in life and overcome the anxiety.

There are in all 18 chapters and 700 *slokas* in it, which covers different topics of yoga (the science of seeking God). Bhagwad Geeta has been translated in most of the languages of the world. Bhagwad Geeta provides a brief but condensed knowledge of many different paths of Yoga like *Sankhya* (Knowledge) *Yoga, Karma* (Action) *Yoga, Bhakti (Devotional) Yoga, Hath Yoga* and the most important the **Kriya Yoga** etc.

2. **The Lessons on Self-Realization**, by Sri Paramhansa Yogananda is a set of sacred literature on seeking God. These lessons provide us, *step-by-step practical detailed instructions on science of Kriya Yoga and Meditational Techniques.* Sri Yogananda himself has written all these lessons, in most systematic and scientific manner for the benefit of God seekers.

These lessons are very useful and convenient to yogis, as these are practical in nature and can be studied and practiced, sitting at home at our convenient time. If someone read and practiced these lessons, then there is no need to leave his sweet family and home, to leave his job and to live in Guru's ashram in his physical presence. All these may disturb the life of God seeker and his family too. A true seeker of God should do his duties to God as well to his family and society also.

3. **The Autobiography of a Yogi**:
   by Sri Paramhansa Yogananda

This is the rare autobiography of a self-realized yogi available in the world. Most of others books are biographies of yogis not written by themselves. It is Yogananda life story with an absorbing account of his singular search for Guru, Truth and God. It is skillfully interwoven with scientific explanations of the subtle but definite laws, by which yogis perform miracles and attain self-realization.

It has been translated into more then 14 languages of the world and is used as an authentic textbook and a reference book of yoga in most of the colleges and universities throughout the world. It gives us the glimpses of the great miraculous gurus & saints of the world, mainly the Jesus Christ and Sri Mahavtar Babaji.

The main aim of this book is to understand the real aim of life of a yogi and how to achieve it? After reading this book, you will be convinced that the main aim of life is self-realization to know God and nothing else. Why do the saints and yogis renounce their families and worldly pleasures, because they are hankering after seeking God?

Some Useful Points to Achieve Self-Realization

All of us dislike any kind of bondage. But we all expect honor, prestige, praise and favor from others. How strange it is? All these expectations lead us to bondages. He, who expects anything from others, is bound to be a slave of expectation. All kinds of such bondages are great hindrance in God-realization.

Remember that God is free from all kinds of bondages. So long we aspire worldly things, we cannot aspire to God-realization. So we must give up our desires for aspiring the worldly things. We should not expect any kind of favor, benefit or praise from others.

If we have any desire, it is a weakness in us. It is an indication of spiritual poverty. Why do we invite poverty for nothing? We should not expect anything from others. It leads us to bondages. We should not demand or expect any worldly thing from God also.

One should not depend upon such things, which are subject to change or destruction. Our real self is eternal, immortal and does not subject to decay or death. One who expects benefits from others is not a rightful claimant. One who wants honor or prestige from others does not really deserve it. On the other hand one who deserve honor and prestige does not hanker after it.

Running after material things produces discontent. The desires have no end. If we become the slave of our senses, the desires will not leave us till our death. The desires are like unquenchable thirst. Only the intense love for God and deep meditation can make you desireless, while doing all your duties in this world.

He who hankers after honor and prestige is slave of these and is not worthy of it. Even if a saint hankers after a disciple or wealth, is a slave of his disciple or wealth. He who has no desires and no craving for any kind of thing is the king of kings. Even the kings have so many desires to be fulfilled and are not free from bondages.

We want a thing only until we have it. When we get the thing the pleasure diminishes. We find that after some time our joy from getting it is gone or lost. Very soon we will forget that it was once our desire. The joy of fulfilling any desire is short lived. But the joy or bliss of communing with God is everlasting. So we must seek God for everlasting joy and not a temporary joy or entertainment from worldly things.

"The human soul is a spark of the Divine Fire. It is immortal, ever conscious, free from impurities, and is blissful."   *...(Manas—7/116/1)*

"Brahman is one, all pervading, omnipotent, and immortal. It is ever-present, conscious and blissful."
                                            ... (Manas—1/22/3)

In fact both soul and *Brahman* are same. The only difference is that soul is separated from *Brahman* by the ignorance of the soul due to *Maya*. Try to get rid of the clutches of *Maya*.

We take delight in eating, drinking, sleeping, talking, watching TVs, and idle rest on bed. But we do not have any time and the same delight to love, pray and worship God. We have been given only one mind and one brain. We may devote it to any thing we like. God has given us freedom whether we devote it to God or to worldly pleasures. Only the right decision, the extreme love and devotion to God, can help us to distract our senses from the worldly pleasures and desires.

A seeker of God must exclusively devote some of his daily time to the pursuit of God-communion. He should not get himself entangled much in the favorable or the adverse circumstances of his life in the world. Otherwise it will become a great hindrance in seeking God. We must give us our deepest love and true devotion to God.

We should totally surrender our heart, mind and soul to God Almighty. We must seek Him in our actions and in meditation. In Bhagwad Gita (VI: 30) Lord Krishna has said: *"He who perceives Me everywhere all around and behold Me in everything. He never loses My sight, nor do I ever loose the sight of him."* So always seek God.

There is nothing more substantial to achieve in the perishable world except God-realization. It is our mere delusion to feel satisfied in achieving wealth, health, honor, prestige, victory and comforts etc. in the world. It is nothing but deception of our ownself. If we die nothing will accompany with us except the fruits of our past actions and the achievements of God-realization.

To achieve or acquire wealth, honor and prestige, we have to indulge ourselves in dishonesty, cunningness, cheating and deceiving others. For indulging ourselves in sins committed, we have to suffer from the fruits of our past actions (*karmas*). Without washing out the fruits of all our karmas (actions), no self-realization or salvation is possible.

None of our worldly wealth or achievements will come to our rescue, when we breathe our last. We are simply wasting our precious time in trying to acquire huge worldly things. Rather we should devote our lifetime to seek and to know God. Remember we should not always think of the comforts and entertainment of this life, but think of your life after death.

From all above, I do not mean to say that you should stop working at all and do nothing for your livelihood and life achievements. But there should be a proper balance of time for all the activities of your life. You should devote your time to worldly things, which are absolutely necessary for an honorable and pleasurable life. But side-by-side you must devote some of your time daily exclusively for seeking God.

There is a great difference between *what we need, and what we desire.* Needs are those worldly things, without which we cannot survive in the world, like good food, air, water, clothes, shelter, education, medicines and sufficient money to lead a comfortable life. We should have that much of money so that we need not to beg anything for our livelihood from any body.

Desires are innumerable, endless and are creation of our own mind. Desires cause bad habits. One may have a lot of un-necessary desires, which are not necessary for the sustenance of his life. A yogi should not have any desire except to know God. Remember that desires can be controlled and minimized by regular *Satsanga*, meditation, reading good spiritual literature and intense devotion to God.

A yogi should not worry about his future. *Future is unknown.* It is in the hands of God. We do not know, what is the best for our future and for present. Only God knows what is the best and what we shall need for our future. We should surrender completely all our desires and needs to God. *God will take care for all our needs, only if, we completely surrender to Him.*

Always remember: *"When every thing is lost, our future still remains."* So never be discouraged or disheartened, if the things are not according to our plans. Whether we are under pleasurable or miserable circumstances, we should have no feeling of pride or aversion for them. We should be indifferent to pleasure and pain. We are already entangled in this duality of pleasure and pain. This is our grievous error due to *Maya*. We should keep on realizing this error.

By complete surrender, I do not mean to sit idle and do nothing in your life. You should do all your duties assigned by God in this world, but do not have any desire to have the reward of your actions. You have given only the freedom of action, but the reward is kept in the hands of almighty God.

"He, whose mind is undisturbed in the midst of sorrow and is free from eager and desires amid pleasures...is called a yogi or sage of settled intelligence. Whatever pleasures are born of contacts with worldly objects are only the sources of sorrow."   ...(Bhagwad Geeta: 2/56 & 5/22)

Due to the development of Tele-communication and electronic media, human beings are now exposed to great events & happenings throughout the world. Naturally the viewer is excited and un-necessarily involved in such events. The seeker of God should avoid such involvements. He should observe the events in such a way, as an observer of a movie keeps him away from his indulgence in the movie. While you are awake, be detached (not inactive) from all worldly activities, things and happenings. This will help you to maintain equanimity of your mind in the midst of sorrows and sufferings.

"He who neither loathes nor desires, should be known as one, who has ever the spirit of renunciation; free from dualities he is released easily from bondage, O mighty armed Arjuna."   ... (Bhagwad Gita 5/3)

Constant *Japa* is very useful in seeking of God. *Japa* is a Sanskrit word. It means to utter the name of the Lord repeatedly either mentally or in a very low voice. *Japa* means the adoration by repeating reverently God's name as a sacred mantra. God is adored by His innumerable names symbolizing His positive and negative qualities. *Japa* reveals both the positive and negative aspects of God. *Japa* insists on the ultimate truth of oneness of Supreme Being with the soul. Remember that the Supreme God may manifest itself in various forms, shapes, and colors, but ultimately it is one.

God manifests Himself as many, yet He is one. He is both the Beauty and Truth. He is the Creator, Savior, Destroyer, Chastiser and Merciful. He is the inner light and essence of all the incarnations, prophets, kings, saints, messengers and all the gods. He strikes fear in no one, yet He is always fearless. He is manifested in everything still He is unmanifested and unchanged. He is Knowledge and *Maya* (Ignorance), the darkness and the light, and the quarrel and the peace. These may look contradictory to us but God is above all these contradictions.

After the realization of God, there shall remain nothing more to do anything. Once we are awakened in God, we are awakened forever in God. As we have to do nothing to learn to awake from our sleep or to sleep from awakening, similarly we have to do nothing to enter *the kingdom of God* from the material perishable world & again come back after the self-realization.

Understand that God didn't create this world just for the people to indulge in human emotions. God also created *Maya* or devil (*Satan*) too. Devil has further created temptations and ignorance. *Maya* has separated creation from the Creator. God is watching and testing every one of us, every moment, whether we are tempted with his creation or to love and seek the Creator.

To convince us about the non-reality and the delusion of the physical universe, God is giving us daily experience of the dreams during sleep to attract us towards Him. God always knows that He is throwing us into the worldly troubles, but remember He also suffers too, due to our troubles. God has imposed the same rules on Himself as on us. God also seeks our love too & suffers if we ignore Him.

Do not think too seriously about the reality of the world and this life. This life is short and will end very soon, before we will know it. All the wonderful past dreams of our childhood & youth have already forgotten by us. Since we do not know our last breath, therefore in the remaining part of our life we must always remember Him. If we seek God earnestly with devotion, how can He remain away from us, and ignore our love? We should constantly and inwardly remember & whisper with Him always. If you give your soul call, He cannot remain away from you.

Our Pride and Ego are our Greatest Enemy and Barrier to Wisdom

Our Ego 'I' (*Ahankar*) is the *cause of our pride, which is our greatest enemy in the world.* Due to our false pride generally we think that we are correct and others are wrong. We do not want to understand and learn from others about their useful experiences. It is a great hindrance in getting more knowledge. It is due to our Ego 'I', *Maya* and ignorance that we think we are the sole doer, in the Cosmic Drama of God.

Sometimes our successes in worldly affairs & achievement make our ego stronger. Due to ignorance we often say that my house, my father, my mother, my property, my children, my bank-balance, my intelligence and my mind etc. All these leads to our false conclusion that whatever we possess in this world is due to our own efforts and intelligence. God has nothing to do with these achievements. Due to delusion we also think that only we are correct and others are wrong. In fact the *truth is just opposite to it.*

The universe around us is the great Cosmic Drama played by God and we are just the actors or images in this universal *movie house.* We do not know, what shall be our role tomorrow and what was our role in our past lives and when we shall leave this temporary hotel on this earth? We shall be deprived to take any thing with us, even our next breath, a penny, our dear ones and even our own physical body,

which is very dear to us. *Remember, we have to leave every
thing all of a sudden against our will.* We don't know our
next destination of our journey after our death. We do not
know what will happen to us at the time of our death. We
daily see others dying and leaving the earth all of a sudden.
But due to our ego and impact of *Maya,* we do not want to
accept the reality that we will also have to leave this earth
very soon.

In our past lives we have already experienced so many
births and deaths, but we have forgotten those due to our
ignorance and *Maya.* Even if we come to know that some of
the persons are able to remember their past lives, we
intentionally ignore them and do not believe them for no
valid reason. It is most unscientific.

All Thoughts Are Coming From God

Do you know that all our thoughts are coming from the
Cosmic Ocean of Knowledge from God? All the streams of
thoughts are coming to our mind from the great reservoir of
Ocean of Thoughts recorded in ether. Due to *Maya* the stray
thoughts distract our mind away from God. To know and
realize God we have to stop this stream of thoughts coming
to our mind from cosmos and become thoughtless. God
listens to the language of our heart in the depth of our
silence of mind and need no other human language. A
thoughtless mind is like a peaceful lake.

But thoughts make our mind turbulent and restless. Then we
are unable to see the bottom of the lake and the reflection of
our own Self in the lake. But when our mind becomes
thoughtless and peaceful, the lake of mind becomes silent.
Then the reflection of our ego 'I' is visible clearly in the
lake.

Do not agree and believe that God is far away from us and doesn't respond to our prayers. Rather, God is closest to our soul and the ego 'I'. God listens to our deep prayers everywhere at all the times, but some-times He answers differently than our expectations. No doubt God answers our prayers, but we are unable to receive it, unless we tune our mind properly to God. If we first tune our mind properly with God during deep meditation, and then pray from heart, we will surely be able to listen His response. We should not doubt on it but practice more and more.

Love and Devotion to God are Must for Self-Realization

It is said that Education without Character, Commerce without Morality, Science without Humanity, Politics without Principles and **Yoga without Devotion is not only useless** but also dangerous to society.

If you want you can practice all the teachings and instructions of yoga without any love & devotion to God. It may also benefit you most in your life, like sound health and sound mind. But if you do not have any love and devotion to God, you may misuse your achievement against others and you will never be able to seek God.

Unless and until you have an intense fire of devotion to God, God will not reveal Himself to you. He loves us all. He is waiting and standing at the door of our consciousness, to enter our heart, but we do not allow Him to let in our heart. Remember *God also suffers, if we deny our love to Him.*

It is a big question, why should we suffer *disappointments* in our lives? Many times it is noticed that we get so much comforts, love, prestige, children and wealth etc. in our life from God. But all of a sudden all these are taken away from us as in case of sudden deaths, accidents, diseases and business losses. The cause is, we have also betrayed God in our life.

In the similar way we have disappointed God, because He loves us and waiting for our love but we have denied our love to Him. Remember, *God suffers too, caused by the separation of our soul from Him and due to our indifferent attitude to Him. Why we have denied our love to Him?*

> *"All things betray thee, who betrayest Me."*
> ...The Hounds of Heaven, Francis Thompson

Science has informed that all object are inflammable, but a minimum **ignition temperature** is required to ignite an object and a minimum amount of escape velocity or **escape energy** is needed to escape an object from earth gravitation or to escape an electron out from its orbital. Similarly a *minimum intensity of meditation fire*, love and devotion is needed to contact with God. But God is not indifferent to any body.

All our prayers are recorded in the heart of Supreme God (known as *Hiranyagarbha*). God will definitely answer to you at the right time. But if you are not able to listen to His answer, do not doubt upon Him and don't be discouraged also. Try to introspect and find out your *own shortcomings if any* and do your sincere efforts with stronger will, devotion and more energy.

Stop doubting and questioning God. These will never end But once you experience God, all your questions and doubts will vanish immediately. The ignorance and the darkness on soul cannot stand before the Knowledge of God. Some may argue, how can he feel love for an unknown God? But if you start loving God, you will immediately get a response.

Let us eat, drink and marry now. Such a philosophy is a waste of the precious life. A doubt without any base is our biggest enemy. If God offers a glass of *Amrita* (the divine drink which makes the soul immortal) to us out of His love and grace upon us, but if some one creates a false doubt in our mind that the glass contains poison, then we will be deprived of drinking the *Amrita*. Isn't it? So never doubt on God without justification.

Do not be Afraid of God

God is the most *beautiful and lovable entity* in the universe. God is not an embodiment of fear as generally presumed. Many think that God is like a man sitting on a thorn in the heaven and God must punish the guilty immediately if some one does any thing wrong. But God waits, watches, and punishes the guilty once when so many of his guilts are accumulated. If God begins to respond and punish the guilty immediately after his sin, God would have become an embodiment of fear like a devil and not the embodiment of love and worship.

But don't think any body can escape from the punishment of his sins and His omni-watching eyes. It is a fool's paradise to think of escape from the fruits of your sins. So you must always talk and whisper to Him. He is always with you and you should never afraid of Him. As a newly born child always feels safe in the lap of his mother, similarly you will not be afraid of anybody, if you are convinced that God is always with you. If you are afraid of your past misdeeds then *try to repent for your sins in the core of your inner heart. Pray God to forgive you for your sins and you should also not commit more sins in your life.*

We have **come alone** temporarily on this earth and will go alone without our asking. We are **living alone in the big crowd** of people around us. The crowd includes even our wife, children, family members and friends. None else on this earth will be responsible for our past misdeeds, not even our wife and children, for whose comforts we have been doing misdeeds in the world. God is not far away from His creation. He is always with all of us. He is present in everything, as ether is omnipresent throughout the universe. God does not need a physical body or a vehicle to be with us.

Do not be Afraid of Death

Every body including a king, a V.I.P., a wealthy man or a healthy man is afraid of death. *Death is inevitable to all.* There is only one reality i.e. God. You shouldn't *be afraid of death,* if God and Guru are with you. If you are awakened in God now, both will be with you at the time of your death. We shouldn't worry anything, if God is with us.

The fear of death is due to our ignorance and inexperience of death. If someone once gets the experience of death in his life, and keeps it remembering, then fear of death his will go automatically. We are not afraid of sleep as we have a daily experience of sleep. *Death is just as good as permanent sleep, but we have forgotten the experience of our past deaths.*

Our **birth and death** are the two most important events in our life. These are the two faces of the same coin i.e. life.

We make all kinds of efforts, preparation, planning, timetable and management for all the important events of our life like: first joining of the school or job, examinations, our marriage, birth of our child, marriage of our children etc. But do we ever bother and thought, about the preparation, management and planning of the most important event of our life i.e. death which is certain one day and our next birth?

You should always think: what will happen to me at the time of my death and what will happen after my death? Where shall I go after the death? Will I take any rebirth? If so, in what form and where will I take birth? Will I take birth as a human or an animal or some other creature? What after that? Is any thing more important for us, than the answers of these questions? Will science help us to answer these important questions, which are haunting the humanity, since millenniums?

As soon as a yogi gets the answers to these questions, in this life during samadhi and then he is not afraid of his death. Many advance yogis gets the experiences of death of his physical body and he again comes back to his physical body. After that he is not afraid of death. For such a yogi death is just a sweet sleep and to replace the old diseased body with a new physical body.

If you are *not awakened in God* and are given the, whole wealth and kingdom of the world and the universe, very soon you will become bored of it. You will not remain happy forever with that kind of achievement. Contrarily, if you have nothing, but are in communion with God, you are always ever blissful, happy and need nothing else.

Don't think that *I am not fit for the spiritual yogic life. Do not believe that to seek God or to know God is impossible* for you. This is the greatest impact of *Satan* or *Maya* on you. The greatest *weapon of Maya is to separate or keep the man away from God.*

Maya creates a false reasoning in our mind and makes us believe that we are not fit to commune with God. To keep *Satan* away from us, try to have the company of God seekers and the Holy *Shastras.* A yogi should never sleep without meditation at night. He should feel the presence of God everywhere in all the things. Throughout the day and night in each of your breath talk and whisper with God. *"O my Father, Thou art always with me in my heart. Do not play the game of hide & seek with me any more. Reveal Thyself."*

Om Anandam Om

5

Techniques of Meditation

Prayer

Maharishi Patanjali Yoga-Sutras:
  Yama, Niyama, Asanas, Pranayam,
  Pratyahara, Dharana, Dhyana, Samadhi

Kundalini Shakti the Spiritual Energy for Involution

Types of Samadhies

Relation of Yogi with God

What Happens during the Meditation

When and How to Meditate

Concentration is Different from Meditation

Devotion & Love are Must for God

Never Forget God

5

Techniques of Meditation

Prayer

O Divine Father! O Guru of all the gurus! O Creator of the delusion and *Maya,* teach me to practice the easiest and fastest scientific techniques of meditation. My naughty mind is always flooded with wavering unwanted thoughts. Teach me to control the unwanted thoughts of my mind in the depth of silence during meditation. Teach me to control at my will the reception and flow of Thy cosmic life energy in my body. Teach me to cut off my five sense telephones from my body and naughty mind, at my will.

From the time immemorial I was separated from Thee, through my ignorance and I have forgotten Thee. But now I have realized that Thou art my ownself, my Mother, my Father, and my goal of life. O, Mother I can wait for unlimited time for any worldly petty thing, but not without knowing Thee. I have left with no worldly desire except to know Thee at the earliest in this life.

Divine Mother! Pity on me, reveal Thee in the temple of my silence and remove the curtains of my ignorance to see Thy beautiful face. I know that Thou art hidden just behind my ego and *Ahankar.* Make me free from the bondage of repeated birth, death and rebirth. I am tired of these. Put me in Thy lap of infinite Ocean of Joy, Bliss and Peace forever.

Yog-Sutras of Maharishi Patanjali[*]

This chapter deals with the scientific techniques of yoga and meditation as told by **Maharishi Patanjali**. About four hundred years A.D. of Jesus Christ, Maharishi Patanjali has given the **eight** necessary steps of *Yog-Sutras* or Aphorisms of Yoga. He has defined Yoga as: *Yogash-Chitvirti-Nirodha*. It means in yoga, *chitvirtis* are to be stopped. *Chitvirtis* are the stream of thoughts in our mind. When the mind becomes thoughtless and peaceful and cut its connection with the five senses and become unaware of the physical body, then it is said to be in the state of **Meditation**.

In this state of consciousness, only the observer or his ego or the self is remained, and everything else vanishes. The observer is situated in his·ownself and observes himself without using any of his sense organ. It is a wonderful state of consciousness with ananda, bliss and joy.

         ... (*Patanjali Yogdarshan: Samadhipad*-I: 2,3,4)

To achieve self-realization faster & without any problem all the *Yog-sutras* are to be followed in an ordered sequence as follows. And none of the sutra is to be ignored.

1. *Yama:* A yogi should observe his moral code of conduct and restraint himself from its violation. This is known as *Yama*. A yogi must observe the rules like: non-violence truthfulness, honesty, chastity, non-covetousness, non-acceptance of others possessions. He should love all, help the poor, never over-eat, observe regular fasting and should have the sympathy to sorrowful and in miseries etc.

---

[*] For detailed practical knowledge of eight aphorisms of Maharishi Patanjali read the book "Kundalini & Kriya Yoga" by Sri Dharam Vir Mangla.

2. *Niyama:* *Niyama* is the personal virtue and disciplining himself by a yogi. A yogi should develop the good habits like: contentment, purity of thoughts, control over speech and action; study of scriptures and *Shastras,* self-denial and above all devotion to God. A yogi should attend *Satsanga* and serve the poor and needy people.

3. *Asanas:* A yogi should practice regularly different kinds of *yog-asanas* (postures) and some light exercises daily. The asanas promotes and facilitates the flow of life energy in different parts of the body organs. Asanas keeps our body free from diseases, healthy and fit to meditate for a long time. Only a healthy body and healthy mind free from all kinds of diseases can go to a state of deep meditation. A sick body and sick mind is unable to co-operate with the strain and stress of long meditation.

The cause of sickness and malfunctioning of some of the organs of our body is due to the lack of life force in some body organ. The distribution of life force is disturbed due to the wrong postures and idleness of the body. But by different kinds of *asanas*, postures and light exercises we can send the life force, forcefully in every part of the body.

There is a great misconception about yoga-asanas among most of the beginners, who think that only the *asanas* practice, is yoga. It is true that asanas are very important, to keep our body and mind healthy and free from diseases. But the practice of different postures or asanas alone has nothing to do with the communion with God, which is the ultimate aim of Yoga.

Asanas are enough to most of the persons in the world, who are interested only to keep their physical body healthy and sound. But *asanas* alone are not enough for seekers of God. Many persons practice *asanas* regularly, and think themselves as a great yogi. It is a great misconception. *Asanas* are only the third step in the eightfold path of Patanjali *Yog-Sutras*.

Lord Krishna is known as the **Lord of Yoga** and the Lord Shiva is known as the **Lord of Yogis**. The words Yoga and Yogis have different meaning. There cannot be any Yoga without devotion to God. To illustrate this I would like to tell you the following. In India there are many organizations in the name of Yoga. Some provides a free training of *asanas* and *pranayam* to every body, in the open parks every morning. They are doing a great service to look after the health of people. They provide a training of group *asanas,* which are useful to keep our body healthy. But most of them ignore God and talk about only the fitness of the physical body to make it free from all kinds of diseases.

It is strange that none talks about the devotion and communion with God. The entire activity of their classes is concentrated on various asanas. None speaks to create devotion to God. What kind of yoga classes are these?

Once a man questioned them for their missing devotion to God. Their reply was strange: "Most of the people are interested only in curing their diseases. They do not come here to seek and commune with God. The members of the organization belong to all the different religions. Some of the members dislike any talk about God. They do not like to prey God, different from their own religion. So to avoid any confrontation, we have better **shunted out God** from our classes and we do not talk, seek and bother about God for the shake of increasing and pleasing our members."

It is similar in other countries also. In some countries the asana teachers are minting money in the name of Yoga. What type of yoga classes they are conducting, without any talk & devotion to God? Most of the books written by them in the name of "Yoga" are flooded in the bookshops all over the world, concerns only with different kinds of asana postures as a cure to different diseases. Such books are really not the books on Yoga. *For a seeker of God it is better to be alone, than to mix with a crowd without any devotion and concern to God.*

You will appreciate the theme of the following interesting but imaginary story: "Once a black red-Indian Christian faithful and devoted to Jesus Christ was forcibly asked to go out from a Catholic Church, by some of the white Christians. The poor black Christian was mentally hurt and suffered with deep sorrow. He wept alone sitting outside the Church for a long time, but none bothered about him.

After some time, a strange handsome bearded man came to console him. He was very much loving and sympathetic to him. He asked him the reasons for his sorrow and consoled him. The black man told him the entire unpleasant incident happened with him. The strange man sympathetically consoled him and said, "Dear son, do not weep and do not worry any more. I am with you always and I have also been thrown out from this Church." The black-man requested him to tell, who he was? The strange old man said, "*I am the Jesus Christ my son.*"

What I want to convey here is, some times we give more importance to our organization and its organized activities but ignore God at the cost of organization. But a real yogi who is the seeker of God is not attached to any organization at the cost of ignoring God. He never forgets his main aim of life to seek God and to know God. He never continues to keep himself attached to any organization, which ignores God and where the devotion to God is missing.

4. Pranayama: The science of willful control of reception, expense and distribution of the cosmic life energy, through the control of breath is known as *Pranayama*. It purifies our body, blood, the nervous system, mind and the brain cells. It also purifies our *ethereal body*. By its regular practice, life force begins to flow freely through our *Nadis (Ida, Pingla & Sushumana)*. Our mind becomes free from distracting thoughts. A thoughtless and peaceful mind is must to achieve the deep state of meditation. This is a misconception that air contains prana or life energy. Air does not contain prana, but simply contains oxygen, Nitrogen and other gases. Prana is present throughout the universe and in my opinion the recently discovered dark energies in the universe are Prana and Kundalini energies etc.

Breathing exercises are also not the *pranayam*. The *Prana* is the omnipresent cosmic life energy of God and we receive it through the medulla oblongata. Through proper inhalation and exhalation we can control our thoughts, which increase the reception and reduce the expense of prana energy. Through pranayama exercises[1] we send the life energy forcibly by our will to any part of our body.

5. Pratyahara: The withdrawal of our consciousness from the outer physical world and to cut off the connection of our five sense telephones from the mind and the sense organs of

---

[1] For details about Prana read the Chapter: Life force doing infinite works for us from "God & Self-Realization".

the physical body is known as *Pratyahara*. Pratyahara is the regular practice of interiorization of mind and its withdrawal from the out worldly distracting things and thoughts. Slowly our mind becomes peaceful and turns from extrovert to introvert. Our awareness is turned inward, away from the distraction of the five enchanting senses. The mind turns toward higher inner spiritual states of consciousness. Such a state of higher consciousness is known as *Pratyahara*.

6. Dharana: *Dharana* means concentration on a single thought. Thousands of stray unwanted thoughts always distract our mind from our goal. We try to focus or concentrate our mind & awareness on a single thought or an imagination of an object. It may be a part of our body, or a picture or a thought of God, or sound of Om, or a pure thought or an imagination. By regular practice a yogi is able to fix his mind for a long time on a single object or thought and turn away all stray thoughts, which distract his mind.

Many yogis begin to learn the art of concentration, by focusing their mind on a candle flame or a small luminous object. After some time, the yogi closes softly his eyes and tries to visualize the same inside his inner vision. His mind just becomes a peaceful observer/ viewer and simply watches the thoughts coming in or going out to the mind. If any stray thought comes to his mind he should let it go away just ignored, without any struggle of his mind. This activity of mind is known as *Dharana*.

7. Dhyana (Meditation): If a yogi is in the continuous state of thoughtlessness with awareness for quite some time, he is under meditation. In the state of *Dharana* mind is fixed on a single thought or an object for quite a long time. By a constant practice the yogi tries to get away this single thought, then his *mind becomes peaceful free from all kinds of thoughts and distractions.* But even then the sense of ego · 'I' remains in his mind. During the state of meditation *(Dhyana)* the yogi forgets his body, cut off the connection of his sense telephones and the mind awareness, but he knows that he still exists.

In this state of consciousness yogi does not have the awareness of any space, time and place, but only his ego 'I' remains, to watch & observe his wonderful state of bliss and joy. Everything else melts away. Breathing becomes dead slow. The heartbeat becomes slow. But the yogi is still aware of his ego 'I' or *Ahankar.* A yogi may listen so many *Anahat* sounds during meditation state and he may try to concentrate upon *Anahat* sounds them to achieve *samadhi.*

8. Samadhi: When the yogi's ego 'I' merges with God or the transcendence of his soul consciousness with Cosmic Consciousness, it is called *samadhi.* In this state of higher consciousness there are extraordinary subtle experiences of subtle worlds. This is the state of *Ananda* (eternal Bliss & Joy) and yogi is in communion with God. It is so joyful that a yogi wishes to remain in this state forever. He becomes free from all kinds of worldly sorrows & desires. The ignorance of yogi melts away. His *Ahankar* or ego 'I' merges with God. By continuous practicing this state of meditation, *Kundalini-Shakti* is raised one day, which is sleeping in dormant state in the lowest part of spine known as *Muladhar Chakra.* After awakening of the *Kundalini-Shakti* our inner journey or the journey back to God or the Divine Romance with God begins.

All the above eight aphorism of Yoga (*Yog-Sutras*) are to be strictly followed by regular practice. If one practice meditation without practicing *Yam, Niyama, Asanas and Pranayam* one may be in trouble and may not get success to achieve *samadhi*. One should not skip, some of the steps of aphorism (*sutras*) to achieve the goal faster. *Devotion and love for God are must for all for an early success and Satsanga is very useful.*

Those who practice yoga without any devotion for God may become healthy and get the mystical powers too, but he can never commune with God. There are two kinds of *samadhis*: **Sabhikalpa & Nirvikalpa samadhis,** which will be discussed later.

Kundalini Shakti is the Spiritual Energy for Involution[*]

It is the Creative Intelligent Force of God. It is also known as the '*VOoice of Silence*'. The *Kundalini Shakti* mentioned above is different from primary life force or *Prana Shakti.* There are two kinds of Kundalini Energies.

1. Universal Kundalini Energy
2. Individual Kundalini Energy

The Universal Kundalini Shakti is said to be the cosmic force, power or energy of the divine that created the universe and it is constantly evolving and developing new materials, atomic and sub-atomic particles and the different forms of living beings.

Individual Kundalini energy is sleeping in dormant form at *Muladhar chakras* of all men. By regular practice of *Yog-Sutras* and intense devotion to God, one day *Kundalini*

---

[*]For detailed practical knowledge of Kundalini & eight aphorisms of Maharishi Patanjali read the book "Kundalini & Kriya Yoga" by Sri Dharam Vir Mangla.

Shakti can be awakened by the grace of God on yogi. It is generally experienced to yogis as a snake sleeping in two & half round at *Muladhar Chakra.*

It is the divine liquid fire that rushes up through the interior of spine known as *Sushumana* and crosses through the seven/six *Chakras* one by one. *Ida, Pingla and Sushumana* is the three main *Nadis* in our subtle body. Without the awakening of *Kundalini* no subtle or *Samadhi* experience is possible.

Generally dormant *Kundalini Shakti* in Muladhara is spontaneously awakened with the grace of God. If Kundalini is awakened without prior purifying of the body, mind and spirit, it may give a trouble to yogis. Some times its huge mysterious power is uncontrollable by the yogis, as the inner passage of *sushumana* in the spine is blocked and not prepared for it. The danger is less if it rushes upward without any blockade in *Sushumana* but more if it turns downwards or sideways.

But a yogi should not be afraid of awakening of his *Kundalini*, if he is practicing and following all the *Yog-Shutras* properly. So before awakening of Kundalini, he must purify his body, mind and soul otherwise it may give him some trouble. The process of involution (the journey back to God) and spiritual unfoldment starts only after the awakening of *Kundalini Shakti. Kundalini* is an initiation for entry into the ocean of divine knowledge and God's kingdom.

As the *Kundalini* crosses the *Chakras* one by one, there are some subtle mystic inner experiences of other worlds to the yogi and he achieves many *riddhis* and *siddhies* (divine miraculous powers and knowledge). No self-realization is possible without awakening and rushing up all the seven *Chakras* by the *Kundalini Shakti and lastly merging in Sahasrar.* Without awakening of his *Kundalini Shakti* and raising it upto *Sahasrar* there can't be any spiritual *Guru.*

Types of *Samadhies*

Samadhi is the highest step explained in the eightfold step by Maharishi Patanjali in his *Yog-Sutras.* There are two types of *Samadhies. Sabhikalpa Samadhi* and *Nirvikalpa Samadhi.* A *samadhi* is attained when the meditator, the process of meditation and the object of meditation become one with God.

The *Sabhikalpa Samadhi* is the initial stage of God-communion. In this Samadhi the life force is withdrawn from the body and the senses. Mind becomes peaceful, thoughtless & interiorized, but with awareness of ego 'I'. The body just disappears or appears dead. A yogi is fully aware of his body, which remains in the suspended animation state. The yogi's consciousness merges with the Absolute Cosmic Consciousness of God. Yogi is in the state of Bliss, Joy and Ananda. Yogi gets some subtle experiences.

The *Nirvikalpa Samadhi* is a higher achievement than the *Sabhikalpa Samadhi.* Nirvikalpa Samadhi gives us full knowledge of *Brahman,* which further gives us *Moksha* or Liberation of soul from birth and death. In this state the mind is attuned to the contemplation of *Brahman,* with *Brahman. Nirvikalpa Samadhi* is difficult to achieve and can be experienced by only the advanced yogis.

Relationship of Yogi with God

It is important for a yogi to clearly define his relation with God. If yogi has no relation with God, his bond of love with

God will be weak. A Yogi is not a physical body, but simply an *Atma* (soul) and God is *Paramatma* (supreme soul). Both do not posses any physical body and therefore have no sex concept. The sex is related with the physical body and not the characteristic of soul. Our soul is neither a male nor a female.

Most of the yogis develop the following relations with God: Divine Father--son; Divine Mother--son; Supreme Lover-- beloved; Lord—servant (das); *Paramatma--atma*; Swami-- disciple; Friend—friend; God--*gopika*; God and 'I' are one and the same (*'So-Ham', or 'Aham Brahmashmi', or 'Tatvamasi'*) etc. A relation may not be fixed or permanent throughout the life of the yogi. Generally it changes from time to time.

What Happens During Meditation

Meditation is a constant practice to realize and express that pure consciousness is the reflection of the image of God within you. Meditation is a joyful state of mind, when it is perfectly tuned with God. After a fixed concentration of mind for a long duration, mind becomes thoughtless but with awareness of ego 'I'. This state of mind is undisturbed by the five senses and distracting stray thoughts of the outer world. Mind is totally interiorized.

We forget our body consciousness during meditation. We forget about all the demands or necessities of physical body. But we are aware of our ownself. Meditation is like dieing of yogi to the world without dieing of the body. Remember we should not sleep during meditation. During meditation we are neither in this world nor in the sleep world.

In meditation we are able to stop our thoughts consciously, what we do unconsciously every night to sleep. One experiences oneness with God along with bliss and joy. During meditation the heartbeats become slow and blood pressure is lowered. Distracting senses are cut off from the mind. The outer disturbances like noise, smell, touch, taste and vision does not disturb a yogi as during sleep our senses do not disturb.

The yogi's mind becomes like an undisturbed peaceful pond of still water. Breathing becomes deep and slow. Pulse rate is decreased. Body organs start feeling like dead one by one. The digestive system is slowed down. The expense of life energy by different organs of the body becomes negligible. The reception of life energy by the medulla oblongata increases many folds. Tired body cells begin to recharge, by the life force. The life force begins to repair the diseased parts of the body.

When and How to Meditate

Since our digestion becomes slow during meditation, it should be done only when our stomach is empty. The best times are early morning, evening, just before lunch or dinner, and just before sleep. During meditation some electricity is generated in the body, so the yogi should sit, on an insulated, soft and comfortable cushion to cut off his body currents from earth. There should be regularity of practice and punctuality everyday.

During meditation one must have deep devotion for God. Without devotion the achievement is less and useless. Ask your family members not to be disturbed by anybody and even by a radio, T.V., phone or doorbell etc. during your meditation time.

Select a remote, clean, airy and beautiful place in your house for daily meditation at fixed hours. Since the earth magnetic field and rotation has an effect on our mind, it is better to face towards North or East in meditating posture. Sit on a clean, soft and comfortable cushion placed on floor. A cushion helps to keeps the body cut-off from the heat and electric currents from earth, produced in the body during meditation.

You may sit, crossed-legged in a simple comfortable posture (*Sukhasana*) or in *padmasana* posture. For short meditation simple crossed legged is sufficient, but for longer meditation *padmasana* is better, which prevents the body from falling when you forget your body during meditation.

First watch the inside & outside of body thoroughly. If there is any tension in any part of the body relax it. Next lightly close the eyes to cutoff the light distractions of the outer world. Again watch your body thoroughly. If still there is any tension in any part of the body relax it. Then watch your breathing-in and breathing-out. The breath must be deep, long and slow. You should fix your mind on inhale and exhale breaths with association of '*So-Ham*' mantra. Inhale with the mental sound of '*Ham*' and exhale with the mantle sound of '*So*'.

Next watch the thoughts in your mind. Thoughts may be coming in and going out. Your mind may be calm and peaceful. Just watch the thoughts coming in and going out as an un-interested film-observer. Do not indulge in, struggle with & attach yourself with thoughts. Concentrate on the *Aggyia Chakra*, the point between the eyebrows. It is also known as *nasikagra* mentioned in Geeta. *Nasikagra* is the point from where the nose starts, which is between the eyebrows. The other end of the nose is the end point of nose and not the starting point (*nasikagra*). It is a misconception among many yogis. They think just opposite.

Concentration is Different From Meditation

The word concentration has come from concentric circles, which have common centre. Fixing of mind on one object or one thought is known as concentration. It is the tendency of the naughty mind to switch over to different thoughts and objects. A yogi tries to tame & fix his mind on a single thought. If it distracts to other thoughts, bring it back to the original thought. If your mind is able to fix on one object or a single thought for long, you are in state of concentration. It is just like the poring of oil from one bottle to another. Remember; during concentration one should not sleep, but keep awaken continuously.

Now try to get away with the single thought or object of concentration and become thoughtless and objectless. Mind should become blank free from all kinds of thoughts. It is now the meditation state. Your mind becomes thoughtless but has the awareness of ego 'I'. You are neither sleep nor awake, but in between the two states. It is known as '*Turia-avashatha*' (a state of pure consciousness).

There are only two things: The world and the God. Human beings are placed between the two. Other creatures have no concept of God. We feel pleasures by coming in contact with the enchanting worldly things through our senses and develop attachment with them. But a yogi realizes that the bliss and joy in meditation is much more enchanting than all the worldly pleasures.

Due to the impact of *Maya* generally we avoid doing experiment with God, because we have neither ever tasted nor have the knowledge of God. None has ever helped us in developing a devotion and love for God. *If only once we experience the eternal bliss and joy of God during meditation, we will hanker after it for the rest of our life.* One should not doubt on it.

During meditation visualize that the cosmic life-energy is entering our body through the medulla oblongata at the centre of the skull. This life energy is directed towards *Aggyia Chakra*, which further distribute it to other *Chakras* in the *Sushumana* and which further distribute it to different body organs. The prana energy is dispersed into sub-pranas when it crosses through any chakra like the white sunlight is dispersed into many colors when it passes through a glass prism.

Try to *interiorize your mind, look within yourself.* Presume that infinite God is everywhere around you. Try to merge your consciousness into super-consciousness. You can expend your mind through eternity and can go beyond the galaxies. Try to listen to God's inner voice. Whenever we make a mistake God warns us silently. If we ignore His warning, He becomes quite. But when we pay attention to listen to Him, He will guide us. By constantly following His voice, we will be transformed into a peaceful, truly moral person. We should not doubt upon this.

Remember that all the thoughts are coming from God and are stored in the ocean of ether. God knows the course of all our thoughts. Unless and until we *completely surrender* ourself to God, He will not like to reveal Himself to us. When we surrender all our worldly desires to God, God blesses us. You may be very busy throughout the day and much tired, even then never go to bed, without your deepest meditation on God.

Due to the power of *Maya* we perceive ourself as a physical body consisting flesh, bones and nerves etc. This is the cause of our many troubles and sorrows in the world. If we meditate continuously and unceasingly, we can quickly realize that we are not the physical body given to us but the infinite essence of God and we will be free from all our problems, miseries, pains and sorrows. It will also make us free from the bondage of our physical body.

Devotion and Love for God is Must for the Seeker of God

During meditation your devotion & love for God is essential. A spark of this love is expressed in all the living beings through us. Understand that the sexual love is different from the devotional love for God. A sexual love is an animal biological instinct, temporary, selfish and a lust for opposite sex. Without this sex instinct there cannot be a sexual love. Sexual love vanishes during old age. So we must realize the eternal love for God. This is without any sex instinct, so great and so joyful but permanent.

The greatest romance that our soul can have is the romance with the Supreme Soul (God). We have no experience and the idea of this divine romance with the Supreme-Lover. But once we commune with God, we will find God everywhere. We will realize that everything in the universe is nothing but the manifestation of God. In samadhi or deep meditation God comes, whispers, guides, plays, loves and communicate with us. We are the best creation in the universe and the children of God. God loves all His children good or bad.

Remember, God does not need any thing from us, except our devotion and love to Him. Since our creation, He is also seeking and waiting for our love too. God too suffers when we deprive Him from our devotion & love. We should always devote a little bit of our daily time, to sit alone, to meditate and have a romance with God. Sri[2] Radha, Sri Meera, *Gopies,* Sri Chataniya Mahaprabhu, Sri Soor Das and so many other saints are the finest examples of the great divine romance with Lord Krishna.

God is the nearest of the near and dearest of the dear in this crowded illusion-world. We must cry for the love of God as a kid cry for his mother and a miser loves his money. Not even a single breath should go without our devotion to God.

As any body cannot escape earth's gravitation without a minimum escape velocity, similarly God cannot be achieved without our minimum love and devotion for Him. When it is achieved God comes and reveals to us. Only our intense pure devotion & love can commune and imprison God, nothing else. A yogi should develop an intense fire of pure love for God in his heart. You should always affirm that the beloved God is always with you in your heart, while you are working, reading, sleeping, dreaming, meditating or doing any other work or activity.

The perishable world is a big stage of divine drama created by God. God has given only to man (others not) the freedom to act (good or bad). Our love is the only thing that God does not possess. Only our love can bind God in our heart.

---

[2] Sri and not Smt. are prefixed before all the saints & gods irrespective of male or female.

Although God is also seeking for our love, but He will never force us to love Him back. We have the freedom to love God or not. But believe me that God is watching, observing and recording all our actions, even our thoughts every moment.

God enjoys all our good actions but also suffers due to our bad actions or bad karmas. Feel the divine love of God in all human being & other creatures, and carry forward the message of love, peace and service to all.

Never Forget God

In both your good and bad times, never forget God. If something happens against your desire or will, do not blame God for it. All the good or bad events, hardships, failures, successes, achievements, diseases, losses and accidents etc. are simply the fruits of our past actions as per the *karmic-law* created by God and have nothing to do with God.

When your desires are fulfilled and you are enjoying all kinds of worldly pleasures, even then do not forget God. All the worldly wealth, we are getting and enjoying is coming from God, out of His divine love and mercy upon us. Remember, without His divine mercy we cannot take even our next breathe in this world. We should prove our worthiness of His Divine Love.

God's love is eternal, unbiased, universal and all embracing like a universal loving Mother. We do not know that during our past and present lives we might have committed so many sins. Only the intense fire of our deep prayer, repentance and devotion to God can wipe out our fruits of past misdeeds and God can forgive us for our past misdeeds. Since everything in the universe is the manifestation of God

Himself, including all living and non-livings. We must love and appreciate His whole creation too.

Our heart, if pure is the best temple of God. In the depth of silence we can whisper, talk, communicate, and express our feelings & love to God who is sitting in our heart. To convey our feelings to Him and to get His blessings too, no language is needed. The hidden universal silent language of heart does everything.

Om Anandam Om

God-Realization Foundation (GRF)
Aims & Ideals

It is a time for spiritual explosion of knowledge. Man has started thinking and seeking to know God for peace, joy and harmony. But man has also become extremely busy with his duties and responsibilities of life. The explosion in Internet and communication technology has solved this limitation of time. As such an organization like 'The God-Realization Foundation' (GRF) is very much needed in the busy world. Now the seekers of God need not wait for a Spiritual Guru, which is difficult to find and contact. You can get the required guidance and spiritual knowledge just at the click of button of your computer. To achieve this aim, GRF has been established by M/s. Geeta International Publishers & Distributors in India. Sh. Dharam Vir Mangla author of spiritual books on yoga along with other spiritually advanced members has founded GRF to achieve its aims.

The aims and ideals of GRF are:

➢ To provide e-spiritual technical guidance directly at home to the seekers of God, who are unable to join an Ashram personally in the company a realized Guru, leaving his family, office or business to suffer.
➢ To create love and devotion for God in the world.
➢ To provide the true universal broad concept of God and to remove the misconceptions about God by the sciences. To encourage the scientists to speak their opinion and truth openly without fear to the world, who are till now silent about God and the Scriptures.
➢ To suggest new topics for further researches in the spiritual field for the scientists, doctors and technicians on the mystic scriptures and about miraculous powers and siddhis shown by the saints.

➤ As yoga is a universal science for all, the teachings of GRF are secular, universal, non-political and unbiased to any religion or philosophy.

➤ To answer the spiritual questions of its members and circulate it to other members, if it is useful to all.

➤ To conduct e-Spiritual-Achievements Tests for its members after every six months, so that they are able to know their achievements. After qualifying four tests, a member is entitled to receive Kriya-Yoga Initiation (Diksha). Then he will receive detailed knowledge of Kriya technique as given by Maharishi Patanjali. Before this eligibility Kriya practice will not be of much benefit.

➤ To provide more information about the miraculous saints and Holy Scriptures to its members.

➤ To serve the mankind and to bring a spiritual revolution in the world to bring peace, harmony, joy and ananda in the world.

How to become the member of GRF & information regarding future publications

Membership fee for registration is Rs 500/- per year in Indian rupees to be sent at 197, Geeta Apartments, Geeta Colony, Delhi-110031 in favor of 'Dharam Vir Mangla' through crossed Indian Bank Demand Draft or Indian Postal Order payable at Delhi.   **OR**

US $ 20 per year to be sent at 3333, Cabrillo Ave Apt # 118, Santa Clara, CA – 95051, USA in favor of 'Poonam Rani Gupta', through crossed Bank Demand Draft only, payable at Delhi in India.

And inform your e-mail ID and payment sent through **dvmangla@hotmail.com** You will be allotted a registered membership number for all the facilities available under it. You may also order for the books to be published soon.

Glossary

Akasha or ether Ether or space, first of five elements evolved from *Brahman (Om)*, the subtlest form of matter. See ether.

Anahat Sounds The inner sounds without any viberation of physical thing, audible even if you close your ears.

Ananda Bliss, joy. Bliss is considered to be the very substance of God (God is bliss, not has bliss).

Asana Easy, comfortable sitting pose. *Hatha yoga* posture of human body.

Ashram Hermitage or monastery.

Astral body Man's subtle body of light or prana or life force; Man has got three bodies: causal body, astral body and physical body. The astral body has nineteen elements: intelligence ego, feeling, mind, five senses, five instruments of actions, and five instruments of life force.

Astral- world The subtle sphere of lord's creation, A universe of light and color composed of life energy or lifetrons. The subtlest aspect of one's being. That which is without any changes, unmodified, unaffected and timeless.

Atma Individual soul; atma is the unseen basis, the substance of the entire objective world. It is the reality 'behind the appearance, universal and immanent in every being.

Avatar or Avatara An incarnation of God. When God takes human form and play lila.

Avidya or Maya Ignorance. Non-Knowledge.

Aum (Om) The Cosmic sound Aum, which creates and sustains every thing. It is the Word or Holy

	Ghost or Hum or Amin.
Baba	Grand Father. A holy saint or *sanyasi.*
Bhagavad-Gita or Geeta	This means "Song of the Lord" revealed to *Arjuna nearly 3250* years B.C. A must for all Yogis.
Bhagavan	Lord. God. "He who possesses all opulences".
Bhajan	Devotional songs.
Bhakta **bhakti**	A *bhakta* is a devotee, one who has *bhakti* (devotion), virtue, self-control, faith, and devotion to God.
Bharat	India
Brahma	The creator God of the Hindu Trinity, the other two being Vishnu and Shiva.
Brahman	The ultimate, unchanging, Absolute Spirit composed of pure being and consciousness before the creation. The immanent principle, said to have three aspects: creation, preservation, and destruction. The absolute supreme reality Brahman is behind the apparent multiplicity of the phenomenal world.
Causal body	The man as a soul is a causal bodied being. The causal body is composed of 35 idea elements: 19 elements of the astral body + 16 basic elements of the physical body.
Delusion	Dual-vision, An illusion suffered by the whole humanity.
Dharma	Religion of God, Righteousness, duty, code of conduct one of the four ends of human pursuit.
Dhyana	Meditation. Thoughtless consciousness with awareness of ego 'I'.
Diksha	Spiritual initiation, to dedicate oneself.
Dus-karmas	Misdeeds, Bad-karmas.

Dusharah   Festival in India celebrating the victory of
                   Lord Rama over Ravana, king of Lanka.

Dwapara   See Treta Yugas.
Yuga

Ether   It does not mean the ordinary organic
                   chemical. The space between the heavenly
                   bodies and the sub-atomic particles is not
                   vacuum, but it is filled with something
                   throughout the universe and even inside the
                   matter and particles. The whole universe is
                   suspended in ether. Electromagnetic waves or
                   light waves cannot travel in vacuum, needs a
                   medium, which is ether. It is the first and
                   finest manifestation of God in the form of
                   matter and, all the subatomic particles has
                   come out of it. It is still undetectable by the
                   scientists.

Gunas   Primary qualities of a human being: peaceful
                   (*sativa*), active *(rajas)* and dull *(tamas)*.

Grahasthi   Married man who lives with his family.

Guru   Spiritual teacher and a guide to spiritual path
                   for a God seeker.

Hatha yoga   School of yoga, which gives more importance
                   to a*sanas* or yoga postures.

Involution   Involution means going back of the creation
                   back to God. For every process of evolution
                   (going away from God) there is a process of
                   involution. The process of involution is going
                   at all the time. At the end of the universe the
                   whole creation will dissolve back in God.
                   That will be a complete involution of the
                   universe.

Japa, japam   Recitation or repetition of the name of the

	Lord continuously.
Karma	Material activities with fruits of actions.
Karmic-law	The fruits of human actions are as per law of karma. The actions of God (lila) are without any fruits.
Karamphals	The fruits of actions.
Knowledge	Opposite of *Maya* or ignorance, helps in knowing God and absolute truth.
Kriya Yoga	A scientific technique of special pranayam in seeking God promoted by Mahavtar Babaji.
Jivan-mukthi **or Moksha** **or Nirvana**	The God-realized person in whom only the divine vision is active. He no longer has any identification whatsoever with his body. He is one with God.
Jnana or **Gyana**	Knowledge. The *yoga* path in which emphasis is laid on knowledge and discrimination, leading to wisdom, and the awareness of one's identity with the divine.
Jnani **(Gyani)**	He has direct knowledge of the highest wisdom. One who follows the path of yoga. The word is also used to denote: one who has reached awareness of his divine identity.
Jyoti	The light and form of a flame.
Kali or **Mahakali**	A name of the divine goddess mother; the Primal energy.
Karma & **Karmic-Law**	Action; the law that governs all action and its inevitable consequences on the doer; the law of cause and effect, or moral compensation for acts done in the past.
Kundalini	Spiritual energy lying dormant in individuals at the lowest point of the spinal cord. It is different from *prana*. Without awakening Kundalini, there cannot be any process of

involution (journey back to God)

Law of Cause & Effect	Every effect or an event must have a cause. There cannot be any event without any cause.
Laya Yoga	The techniques of concentration on *Anahat* sounds to achieve self-realization.
Leela (lila)	Divine play of an Avatara of God, which are without the fruits of karmas.
Life Energy or prana	Prana, Intelligent cosmic energy responsible for creation and organization of life and matter.
Maha-Samadhi	Willfully leaving the body by the soul of a Yogi (willful death).
Mahatma	A great purified soul.
Mahavtar Babaji	The great grand guru of Sri Paramhansa Yogananda. The Eternal Himalayan Yogi.
Magic	A mysterious performance by using hidden tricks to deceive the viewers.
Mantra	Sacred words or verse repeated during meditation or Vedic hymn.
Mauna	Observing silence.
Maya	Ignorance obscuring the vision of God; the primal enticing illusion appearing as duality and called the world; creates attachment with world.
Mind	The cosmic energy by which the brain functions
Miracle	A mysterious phenomenon generally seems to defy the known laws of sciences.
Mukti or Moksha or Nirvana	Salvation or Liberation of soul free from material existence of birth and rebirth.
Nirvikalpa Samadhi	When experiences total oneness with God & Truth after the death of ego 'I'.

Nirgun & **Sugun**	Nirgun means devoid of any properties (Brahman). Sugun means which have some properties. Nirgun is opposite of Sugun.
Nirvana or **Moksha**	Freedom from material existence. But still may be separate from God.
Om or Aum	The primeval *Anahat* sound by which God sustains the cosmos.
Padmasana	A cross-legged posture for long meditation.
Paramatma	The pure *atma* viewed in its universal aspect as God.
Paramhansa	The highest degree of spiritual achievement of Nirvikalpa Samadhi. Higher then Swami.
Patanjali	The name of the ancient sage who wrote the basic guide to Y*oga,* known as *Patanjali Yoga Sutras.*
Prana	The vital force or cosmic energy that sustains life in the physical body in all living beings. There are five types of *prana.*
Prema	Divine love of the most intense kind, universal unconditional unblemished love. It is different from sexual lust generally called love.
Puranas	Eighteen Holy Books of Hindu *Shastras,* which describes historical events and are supplements to Vedas.
Purusha	Eternal conscious principle; Soul.
Rajsic	The active, passionate aspect like king.
Rishi	A sage, one leading a life without desires, with attachments only to the a*tma.* A seer of truth.
Sadhak	A spiritual aspirant engaged in conquering his egoism and greed, the sense of 'I' and 'mine'.
Sadhana	Spiritual discipline or practice through activities such as meditation and recitation of

holy names.

Sadhu   A holy-man, generally used with reference to a monk.

Sai   The divine mother of all.

Samadhi   It is the highest step on the eightfold path of Patanjali-Yoga. The shuttle experiences beyond delusion and Maya. Samadhi is attained when the meditator or observer, the process of meditation and the object of meditation (God) becomes the same. Trance, perfect equanimity, untouched by joy, sorrows and communion with God. Complete absorption in God consciousness.

Sanyasi &   A Hindu ascetic; one who has adopted the
Sanyias   monastic, celibate life. Wears saffron clothes. Do not live in any family.

Satan   *Maya.* The power by which God has separated Him from His creation.

Self-   When the human soul experiences & merges
Realization with God and *Maya* vanishes.

Shastras   The scripture that illumines, the moral code, directly transferred to humanity from God. Ordinary human mind cannot write *Shastras*, without the grace of God. Only superhuman man writes the Shastras. Shastras are the authority in the spiritual field.

Sat-chit-   The supreme state, usually translated as
Ananda   existence, knowledge, bliss.

Satwik   Pure, good, pious; the principle of balance or wisdom.

Sathya   Truth that which is always the same no matter past, present, future or circumstance

Satsanga   Being in the society of good, spiritual people.

Satwik,   The three *gunas* or characteristics of

Rajas &Tamas	embodied beings, translated roughly as peaceful, active and dull.
Self	*Atman* or soul.
Self-Realization	The state of knowing God, the absolute state of God achieved by yogi, the soul merges in God and all the powers of God like omnipresent, omnipotent and omniscient are achieved Yogis when the body, mind and soul become one with The soul is in permanent Bliss or Happiness or Joy.
Adi Shakti	The creative divine power; a name of the divine mother; the feminine aspect of God, representing power and energy.
Shanti	Undisturbed peace, eternal peace.
Shiva	Adi-Purusha. The destroyer God of the Hindu trinity, the other two being *Brahma* and *Vishnu.*
Siddha/ Sidhpurusha	*A siddha* is one who has attained *siddhies* (yogic *powers).* Individualized Spirit.
Soham	So means He, and ham means I. Soham means He is I or I am He. This mantra is realized in Nirvikalpa samadhi.
Soul	Atma
Sukhasana	A cross-legged easy posture for meditation.
Swami	Lord, spiritual preceptor, a member of India's most ancient monastic order.
Treta Dwapara & Kali Yugas	The second of the four *yugas* or cycles of world periods. Hindu Shastras divides the duration of the world into four *yugas, Satya, Treta, Dwapara* and Kali. The first is known as the Golden Age as there is a great preponderance of virtue among men, but with each succeeding *yuga* virtue diminishes and vice increases. In the Kali yuga there is a

minimum of virtue and- a great excess of vice. We are supposedly in the Kali *yuga* now. It was started after Lord Krishna approx. 5300 years ago.

Upanishad A category of Indian scriptures. 108 philosophical treatises that appear within the *Vedas.*

Vedanta Anta means end of Vedas or later portion of Vedas"; Adi Shankaracharaya was the chief exponent of Vedanta.

Yoga Yoga means communion of *atma* (soul) with God. Yoga is that science by which the soul gains mastery over the instruments of body & mind and uses them to attain Self-realization: the reawakened consciousness of its transcendent, immortal nature, one with Spirit.

Veda The Knowledge of God. The oldest scriptures about God are known as Veda.

Vedanta One of the·six systems of Hindu philosophy, formulated by Bhagwan Ved-Vyas.

Vedas The most sacred scriptures of the Hindu religion, regarded as revelations to great seers and not of human origin. There are four *Vedas:* The *Rig-Veda,* the *Yajur-Veda,* the *Sam-Veda* and the *Atharwa-Veda.*

Vedic Which is derived from Vedas.

Vishnu The preserver God of the Hindu Trinity, the other two being *Brahma* and *Shiva.*

Yoga or Yog Union of the individual soul with God; also the technique by which to realize this union. It is the general term for the several types of devotional practice that the disciplines used to control the mind and transforms it into an

Yogi   instrument for God-realization.
The devotional spiritual aspirant who seeks union with God by means of one or more specific mental and physical disciplines which are traditional and which are known by the title of *yoga*.

Yugas   The four phases of world through which life moves to complete a world cycle. Sat-Yuga, Treta Yuga, Dwapara-Yuga and Kali-Yuga